THE
COLD WAR
AND THE
INCOME TAX

The
Cold War
and the
Income Tax:
A
Protest

by

EDMUND WILSON

FARRAR, STRAUS AND GIROUX
NEW YORK

BOOKS BY EDMUND WILSON

CONTENTS

THE
COLD WAR
AND THE
INCOME TAX

A Bad Case of Tax Delinquency

Between the year 1946 and the year 1955, I did not file any income tax returns. Up to the end of 1943, I had been living for years on a shoestring. In 1941, I had bought an old house in Wellfleet, Cape Cod, Massachusetts, for the now incredible price of $4,000 by borrowing $1,500 and taking out a mortgage for the rest. The house was at this time uninhabitable, and I had to spend at least $1,000 for improvements. I lived in this house with my family all the year around. I was then engaged in writing a book which occupied me for about six years, and I met the bare expenses of living by writing also occasional articles and by compiling a kind of anthology on the history of American literature. At the end of 1943, I was offered a regular job on the *New Yorker* magazine doing weekly literary articles, and in order to meet certain debts which I had contracted while writing my book, I accepted it and moved to New York, where I remained for several years. I was then on a regular salary, and from this, of course, my tax was withheld. My wife and I filed returns at this time.

But by the beginning of 1945, my wife and I had separated. I had gone on a lighter schedule in contributing to the literary department of the *New Yorker*, and I went to Europe as a foreign correspondent for it, from April to September of that year. From this time I ceased to file. Income tax was still being withheld from the salary I was paid by the magazine, and I had very little other income. The book on which I had been working, *Memoirs of Hecate County*, was published in 1946, and I found then, for the first time in my life, that from this book and from my current journalism, I was making what was for me a considerable amount of money. (My top earnings up to then had been the salary of $7,500 that I had had for a few years as an associate editor of the *New Republic*). When I wanted to get married again and had to pay for two divorces, I did not hesitate to use for this purpose the money from the sale of my book. I knew that the profits from the book were to some extent subject to the income tax, but I thought that this obligation could always be attended to later. I had no idea at that time of how heavy our taxation had become or of the severity of the penalties exacted for not filing tax returns. I knew that misrepresentation in one's income tax returns could be used to send to prison a gangster like Al Capone or a swindler like Charles E. Mitchell of the National City Bank, who had been able to cover up the traces of more serious crimes. But I did not know that failure to file also constituted legal "fraud" (both "wilful" failure to file and reporting income falsely are "frauds," but though the latter constitutes a "felony," the former is a "misdemeanor"). From my book that was then selling well I expected a further income, and I should soon, I thought, be able to catch up on what I owed to the government. I did not expect—what soon occurred —that my novel would be suppressed, and my income from it abruptly cut off.

It may seem naïve, and even stupid, on the part of one who had worked for years on a journal which specialized in public affairs, that he should have paid so little attention to recent changes in the income tax laws; but after the death of my second wife, I had resigned from the *New Republic* and reverted to my usual practice, when I did not have to support a family, of devoting myself mainly to my books and getting along more or less from hand to mouth. I had lived from 1932 to 1935 in a little old shabby framehouse at 314 East Fifty-Third Street, which was supposed to be soon torn down and which I rented for $50 a month. It actually cost me less because I could always sublet parts of it to friends. I was working at that time on my "study in the writing and acting of

history" called *To The Finland Station,* which dealt
with the development of Marxism and the Russian
Revolution, and I obtained a Guggenheim Fellowship
in the spring of 1935 for the purpose of exploring the
subject in the Marx-Engels Institute in Moscow. I
was politically suspect in the Soviet Union and was
never during my three months in Moscow allowed
access to the Marx-Engels Institute; but my visit
was invaluable to me in affording me firsthand knowledge of Russia, which I should not otherwise have
been able to acquire. My resources at this time con-
sisted of the tax-free $2,000 which I had from the
Guggenheim Foundation—which the Foundation
generously supplemented when, just as I was leaving Russia, I came down with scarlatina and had to
be quarantined.

This, however, belongs to a period antecedent to
that of the tax delinquency for which I was later to
be prosecuted. But by the time I was married again
in 1946, my financial situation was no better than
it had been in 1936. The earnings from *Hecate
County* had been cut off by the book's suppression.
I was now working on something new, my play
The Little Blue Light. My income for the years 1947–
1951 averaged $2,000 a year. For the years '48 and
'49 I was liable for no tax at all, and I thought that
before filing for the years since 1945, it would be
better to wait until I was making more money. (I

still was unaware that failure to file had been made a serious offense.) This happened in 1955, when a long article of mine on the Dead Sea scrolls was published first in the *New Yorker* and afterwards as a book, and both of these had a certain success. I then went to an old friend of mine, an extremely able lawyer in New York, and explained to him my situation. I found that he was astonished and appalled, and I learned to my own astonishment that I could be heavily fined and sent to jail. This seemed to me outrageous in the United States, where imprisonment for debt was supposed to have been abolished at the time of the Revolution. I learned also for the first time then about the quarterly estimates of future income, the Ruml plan of 1943, with its cheerful slogan "pay as you go"—the tax law according to which you are obliged to pay every quarter an estimated tax in advance on money which you have not yet earned or received. It is of course as a rule impossible for a writer of serious books to have any idea what he is going to make; but if one's estimate beyond a certain point falls short of what one turns out to make, one is penalized for having guessed wrong. My lawyer friend told me at once that I was evidently in such a mess that he thought the best thing I could do was to become a citizen of some other country. This seemed to me at the time fantastic. I had no wish to live abroad; I was more interested in and involved with the United States than I could imagine being with any other country. I told my friend to risk it and go ahead, to prepare and file the returns for the years when I had been "delinquent"; that I was ready to take the consequences. But he thought I should ruin myself—as turned out to be more or less correct—and he worried about me so much, as only an old friend would have done, that he told me that my predicament was giving him more trouble than all the rest of his practice put together. His office made out the returns, and my wife and I signed them and directed him to file them just before going away to Europe. He said as I did so, "You're a brave man!" I had given him a check for $9,000, from the royalties from my book on the Dead Sea scrolls, to offer as a payment on account for my debt. (I had only learned a little while before that one did not have necessarily to pay the whole amount on filing. If I had known that I could file without paying the whole, and that I was incurring heavy penalties by failing to file, I should certainly have filed long before.) But when we came back from Europe a couple of months later, we discovered that nothing had been done, and I was told that the sum I had left was too little to count for anything in averting my annihilation. My friend had been racking his brains for some means of settling the matter in a more satisfactory way, and he suggested various expedients, none of which recommended itself to me. He had at this time had the first of a series of strokes, from which he not long afterwards died, and I was coming to realize that he would never be able to handle the case in court, that he really, in fact, could not get to the point of doing anything about it at all; so I eventually took it out of his hands.

But I did not now know what to do. I had been drawing on the $9,000 for current living expenses, and part of the rest of it went for a fee. The lawyers in New York seemed terrified of the Internal Revenue Service. One of the men in my friend's office had been greeted by uplifted hands and cries of "No deal! No deal!" when he had visited the Manhattan headquarters, and I was told that my case was so bad that no lawyer in Manhattan would touch it without an enormous retainer. I did nothing and went up for the summer to northern upstate New York. One day, coming back from a journey—in June, 1958—I found a notice from the Internal Revenue office in Utica, ordering me to let them know when and where I had last filed an income tax return. I went to a Utica lawyer recommended by a local friend, who generously took my case though I had not a penny then to offer him.

The Delinquent in the Hands of the IRS

It eventually took two lawyers negotiating with
the tax authorities five years to get my affairs settled
—though one would think that once my indebtedness had been assessed and the degree of my criminal
transgression determined, some agreement could
have been sooner arrived at. But demands for impossible sums were insisted upon for years, and then
—contrary to the protestations of the men in the
Manhattan office—the whole thing was closed by a
deal.

First of all, I was liable to prosecution for the
years 1953–1957. There is a statute of limitations on
liability to indictment for past delinquency but, in
the course of tightening up the tax policy, this im-
munity had been curtailed and now did not extend
further than to six years back. If it had been assumed
that my failure to file had been wilful throughout
my delinquent period, I could legally have been indicted for each one of these six years, and I could
have been fined $10,000 for each of them and for
each of them sent to jail for a year. In view, however, of the fact that my signed returns could be

shown in evidence of an intention to file for all except the last of these years (when I had taken the
affair out of the hands of my friend), the authorities
were prevailed upon merely to bring "an information" against me for wilful failure to file in 1957. I
was technically put under arrest, but my lawyer had
engaged to produce me, so the sheriff did not lead me
into court; but I had already been fingerprinted and
catechized by a parole officer, and had had to produce my honorable discharges from the army. I
should perhaps have been grateful to the court that
it accepted my no doubt rather unlikely sounding
story and fined me only $7,500. I had, however, it
might be noted, paid already nine months before
my taxes for 1956 and 1957, which amounted to
something over $16,000.

But now my indebtedness for the previous ten
years had to be taken care of, and it had been calculated that I still owed the government between $68
and $69,000, a sum which had been arrived at by
the slapping on of 6% for interest and 90% for penalties: that is 50% for fraud, 25% for delinquency,
5% for failure to file and 10% for allegedly under-
estimating my income. Having already had to borrow in order to pay the fine, I declared to the officials
in Utica that it was impossible for me to provide
this sum and that unless I should make suddenly a
good deal more money than I had ever done before

in my life, I had no prospect of ever being able to do so. It was not explained to me at the time, as it should have been, that what is called an "offer in compromise" was possible—that is, that I might settle for less. If this had been made clear at this interview, a settlement might have been arrived at much earlier. This failure on the part of the authorities to explain to the delinquent citizen what his rights are in such situations or what measures of reprisal are being taken against him is one of the intolerable features of the despotic IRS system. I was informed for the first time at this interview that the quarterly income from a family trust fund had already been seized by the government. When I complained that I had not been notified of this, I was told that I had been warned, on a printed slip which was sent me in demand of the sum assessed that if I did not produce this assessed amount, I was liable to liens on my property. I was, in any case, now ordered to present to this bureau an itemized monthly accounting of every cent of income I received and every cent I spent for living expenses. When I came for a second interview, after two months of such accounting, I was reprimanded for spending too much money on liquor, for taking my Italian translator to the theater, and for having bought a $6 mat for my dog. I was told that since I myself "had no place to lay my head," I had no business to buy my dog a cushion, the implication being that I myself was allowed a bed only by the grudging leniency of the Internal Revenue Service. In the meantime, without any notification, all my remaining sources of income were shut off by either levy or lien. The IRS agents had looked up all the publishers and editors that I had listed in my tax returns, including several from whom I had received only trifling amounts and those several years ago. In the case of the levy, a tax agent would go into the editor's or publisher's office and demand to receive on the spot any money that might be due me; in the case of the lien, the agent would tell the publisher that he could not pay me anything but must hold any money due me until the lien was lifted. This kept me strapped for nearly a year. I own at the present time, two houses, one the house on Cape Cod that I have mentioned above and the other a family house in New York State, over a century and a half old, which, since buying the Cape Cod house, I have inherited from my mother. There were liens now on both of these, and I was told at one of these interviews that I did not need the family house, since I did not inhabit it regularly—a suggestion that if I did not sell it, the government might well take it away. To add to my offense in the eyes of the government, I had been renting for $200 a month a small house in Cambridge, Massachusetts, where

I had had for a year a job lecturing at Harvard,
where I still needed the Harvard Library for a book
I was then writing and where my daughter was
going to a private school. The tax officials thought
this was indefensible, and one of them told my
lawyer that he himself made $7,500 a year and got
along with only one house and that he didn't see
why I, a tax offender, should have the effrontery to
think I could live in three. And of course a private
school for my daughter was completely inadmissible.
But I had learned with surprise at this interview that
an "offer in compromise" was possible, and the official who presided—though undoubtedly picking a
figure out of the air—mentioned "say, $30,000." I
accordingly made out a form offering $20,000, which
was almost what I owed for back taxes exclusive
of interest and penalties, and at the end of four
months, I was informed that this offer was rejected.
They would tell you, it appeared, what they would
not accept, but at this time it was absolutely impossible to get them to tell you what they would accept. In an endeavor to find this out, I went to Syracuse with my lawyer and called at the office of the
District Director. We were received by the Assistant
Director, a courteous and reasonable young man,
who called in people from various departments to
inform him about the case. One thing had now become clear, though it had appeared rather late in

the proceedings: that they wanted to have my offer accompanied by what they called "a collateral agreement." This meant that though an offer might be accepted for a definite sum paid down, one would have to assign to the government over a limited term of years all one earned or received in income above a certain amount. I refused at the time to do this and tried them with another offer—the full amount of the taxes—which in due course was rejected, too. (I had set aside a certain sum in order to be able to make good my offer, and I knew that if I needed more money, I could borrow it from various sources.)

I again went to Syracuse and for the first time complained and protested. I reminded them that my case had been left in the air for years, while more interest and penalties were rolling up, and that by cutting off my sources of income, they were making it more and more impossible for me even to support my family except by finding some new publisher or editor—which I had made no attempt to do—who, as soon as they found out about him, would also be forbidden to give me money. The Assistant Director, at this second interview, had called in three of his associates: the man who was responsible for the auditing (a different person from the one who had been present at the previous interview, and who had therefore to get the case up again); the man who was responsible for the liens; and the man—he had not been present at the earlier interview—who was supposed to know the facts on my criminal record. I had been struck in the Soviet Union by the incompetence of the Communist bureaucracy and had contrasted it with what I took to be our superior efficiency in performing routine tasks in the United States. In Russia, the bank clerk who cashed your check or the railroad clerk who sold you a ticket was afraid to do even this without consulting someone higher up, and if it was possible, the lesser officials preferred to keep on passing the buck till the applicant gave up hope and no decision had to be made. This was not the case, I thought then, with us. There was a real coöperation here, a real distribution of responsibility. But the clerks behind Soviet wickets were of course employees of the government, and I had never then had very much experience of our own government employees. In the case of these American officials with whom I was now dealing, the trouble was not so much that they did not in their own departments have authority to make decisions but that the work of such an organization as the Internal Revenue Service had been more and more split up and specialized till no one person had any real grasp of all the aspects of any given case. I found that the lien and levy man did not really seem to be informed as to what methods had been applied to the sources of my income, since

these were all in New York City or New Jersey and
were controlled by other agents in the offices there.
Nor, of course, was the problem of how I was to
live any part of his official business. (When my lawyer had brought this up in Utica, he was told,
"We're not concerned with hardship.") For the
criminal record man, it was necessary to tell all
over again the story of the unfiled returns, which had
already been accepted by the court and on which
he did not seem well-posted, since he disregarded
the evidence that the unfiled returns had been made
out in good faith and signed. My impression has
been confirmed by the accounts of other people who
have had similar experiences that when one of these
cases is shifted from one IRS office to another—and
they are constantly being shifted—it loses all its
previous history: nobody knows anything about it;
you rarely see the same person twice. I had been
getting to have the impression that my case could
never be settled because no one who dealt with it in
the course of routine was in a position to sum it
up and settle it. But my appeal that day made
some impression. I felt that for the very first time,
by getting together in one office four men who had
undoubtedly, I thought, never conferred about the
matter before, we had obtained a point of concentration, had struck off perhaps a spark of activity.
The Assistant District Director promised us defi-

nitely that in a very few days some acceptable offer would be indicated.

He kept his word, but the sum demanded— $40,000, I think, plus the collateral agreement—was still impossible for me, even borrowing all that I could hope to, and of course I should have to pay it before the liens and levies would be lifted so as to liberate my paralyzed resources. In the meantime, I had no idea how much of my money had been confiscated and how much had been merely frozen. But I still had the right to appeal; and my lawyers made an expedition to Buffalo to see the head of the Appellate Division there. This official, I understand, insisted on the payment of a sum of the same order as that demanded by the district office in Syracuse, and the matter was left undetermined; but my lawyers, on a second visit, found an unexpected change of attitude and a readiness to accept $25,000, plus a collateral agreement for four years. The authorities, in fact, had ended, after months of negotiation, by accepting—plus the signing of the collateral agreement—a sum not very much in excess of the figure they had been offered in the first place. This was possible for me to meet, but the arrangement had to be confirmed by Washington, and the approval from the headquarters of the IRS did not come through till almost four months later. Then before I could get such money as had not already been attached I had to wait for the levies and liens to be lifted. When this was done, the income from the trust fund turned out to have been omitted, and I had to make further application in order to get this released. When the money was at last made available, I had to pay almost all of it out to the government or to the New York State Income Tax Bureau. It turned out that the collateral agreement, contrary to my expectation, had been made retroactive by a year, so that I had to disburse to the IRS over $5,400 —the collateral surplus—of a special sum of money which I had raised to make good my offer. I was left with about $400 in the bank; an unpaid personal loan of $10,000; a mortgage on one of my houses, and my future literary work mortgaged ahead for over $30,000, so that I should not be able to receive anything for completing and delivering this work till that value had been repaid—which, in the case of the most important item, would very likely take me the rest of my life (as I write, I am sixty-eight); and unpaid lawyers bills of between $8 and $9,000. (My legal expenses in all have amounted to over $16,000, to say nothing of fees to accountants.)

Everybody Is Under Suspicion

When the income tax people first began looking me up, they found that I had been married four times, and this, I was told, was brought up against me. It is apparently un-American to be married four times. Though many people, whose church forbids it, believe that divorce is a sin, it may be said that aside from these groups, two marriages with a divorce are thought normal; among the rich, three are normal; and in Hollywood four are normal. But in the case of a writer, four marriages may throw doubt on his financial dealings and on his soundness as an American citizen.

I do not believe, however, that very much was made of this. My political reputation was more serious. The IRS does not depend for its political information on the espionage of the FBI: it has an intelligence service of its own, the extent if not the accuracy of whose researches surprised me. It was reported that my previous lawyer and I, at the time when he was handling my case, had together attended in Manhattan the trial of an income tax offender and that when we found this offender was

acquitted, we had decided not to file my returns.
It was true that my friend had attended such a trial
—in which, however, I believe that the defendant
was convicted; but I had not been with him, had
not even been in New York, and at the time knew
nothing about it. Then my books were attentively
read, with a view to finding evidence which would
show me to have been a "subversive" character. It
was discovered that in 1933 I had written an article
on the fall of Charles E. Mitchell, and it was put to
me that I knew at this time that one could get into
serious trouble for non-payment of income tax
(though the character of Mitchell's offense was
legally distinct from mine). It was reported that
I had been known in the past for my participation
in "Red" activities, and though the judge who
sentenced me in Syracuse seems honorably to have
disregarded this, I know that it had been called to
his attention, and the idea that I had at one time
been associated with persons who wanted to over-
throw the government by violence gave undoubtedly
a blacker aspect to my failure to report income to
to the government. It was fortunate that my lawyer was able to counter with the demonstrable
fact that my book *To the Finland Station*, which described the rise of Marxism and led up to the Russian
Revolution, had been circulated abroad by the State
Department both in English and in Italian.

That an arraignment for income tax delinquency should involve an investigation of the complexion of one's political opinions appeared to me so absurd in a country that prided itself on political freedom that I told the story to a lawyer in one of the oldest and most distinguished and most respectable Boston firms. He did not express the least surprise. When I had finished, he said: "Let me tell you a story." He had been offered, he said, in the early days of the Eisenhower administration, the post of chief attorney for the IRS in Washington. In indicating his willingness to accept, he explained that it ought to be known that he had rented, when he first got out of Law School, a room in a large New York house belonging to a college friend of his, who was rich but who had Communist affiliations. He did not share this friend's views, and though he had done for him some legal work in connection with real estate, he had never represented him legally in connection with his political activities. But the FBI now took up the lawyer's case and proceeded to send its agents to every street in New York on which my friend had lived, in order to question the shopkeepers about him. This search did not yield satisfactory results, but it was found that his wife was a member of the board of an institution called Literary Intercultural Studies, the reading room of which was frequented by the armed forces, and

which contained informative books about Soviet
Russia—which was true—and reported—what was
not true, since his wife had never written for publication—that she had contributed to the *Daily
Worker*. This investigation went on for three
months, at the end of which time my friend was
officially informed that since he had been found
to be a "controversial figure," he was advised not
to accept the post—which he was by that time very
glad to do. He had previously been assured by Washington that neither his not being a Republican but
being registered as an independent voter nor his
friendship with the Leftist millionaire would preju-
dice his appointment, and, in the meantime, under
the impression that he was sure of going to Washington, he had resigned from his firm in New York.

I later repeated my story, adding to it that of the
lawyer, to a Harvard professor of history, with
high official connections, who had served in the last
war, attaining the rank of lieutenant colonel, and
afterwards in the State Department from 1946 to
1948. He, too, failed to show any emotion. He said
that in 1953, five years after leaving Washington, he
had suddenly received by registered mail an official
communication which ordered him to answer certain charges. These included an accusation that he
had tried to introduce into the federal service, for
purposes of economic research, an economist who

was secretly a Communist. He replied that to the best of his knowledge this man was not at that time a Communist, if indeed he had ever been one. It was also charged against him that he had argued in favor of Communism with an officer of the army. The explanation of this was that the professor, a specialist in European history, had made an attempt to enlighten, on the subject of post-war Czechoslovakia, an assistant air attaché who was being dispatched to Prague and who seemed to him dangerously ignorant of what had been happening in Eastern Europe. The professor fully answered these charges. When he resigned his commission as a reserve officer, he was discharged "under honorable circumstances." But five years later—in 1958—he received, without explanation but with instructions to destroy the old document, a new discharge from the army, which bore the same date as the old one. It now turned out that the previous document had been what was called a "gray discharge"—that is one that appeared to be "honorable" but that actually implied reservations—the suspicion, among others, that the man thus discharged was either a Communist or a homosexual. The professor had received at last, twelve years after retiring from the service, a genuine honorable discharge which gave him a clean bill of health. How delighted and grateful he must have felt!

What Rip Van Winkle Woke Up To

At this point, let us squarely confront, as I had
been failing to do, the tax situation to which I awoke
when in March, 1953, I went to see my friend
the New York lawyer.

What is the history of this tax in the United
States? It is interesting to trace its progress. An income tax was first imposed under Lincoln on July
1st, 1862, when, as a result of the cost of the Civil
War, the public debt was increasing at the rate of
two million a day. This tax was abolished in 1872.
An attempt was made to revive it under the second
administration of Cleveland, in response to the pressure of the Populist movement, that rebellion of the
Western farmers, who had been suffering from a
series of droughts and the competition of grain from
abroad and who were having their farms taken away
from them as a result of foreclosures by the bankers; but this was defeated in the Supreme Court by
a five to four decision, on the ground that such a
tax was in violation of the rights of property and of
the constitutional principal that any direct taxation
had to be collected from the states in proportion to

their population. An amendment to the Constitution was, however, put through in 1913, which authorizes Congress "to lay and collect taxes on incomes, from whatever sources derived, without apportionment among the several states and without regard to any census or enumeration." The present system was now established, and Woodrow Wilson took advantage of it, during his first administration, at first to impose a small tax intended to compensate for the loss of revenue involved in the Underwood Tariff, which was, also, in its way, a popular measure, designed to lower prices by breaking the monopoly of American business. But after our entrance into the first World War, which cost us something like thirty-three billion dollars, the rates of taxation were raised and those of exemption lowered. After the war, these rates were reduced; but, beginning in 1932, they were raised and exemptions were cut in the interest of programs of relief, and when we entered the second war, which cost us three hundred billion, about ten times as much as the first one, and which brought up the national debt to two hundred and forty-seven billion, the rates were raised again to what was so far the highest level in our history. Two-fifths of the total cost of the war was paid for out of these taxes, and the number of persons liable was raised between 1939 and 1943 from four to thirty million. In 1943, the system of quar-

terly estimates was instituted, as well as the withholding system in its present all-embracing form,
which exacts from the employer an appropriate
amount of every employee's salary. After the war,
some attempt was made, in 1948, to relieve this tremendous pressure; but the pace of our frantic
rivalry with Soviet Russia, with its insistence on more
and more nuclear weapons and its hit-or-miss squan-
dering of our money abroad, has been subjecting us
since 1950 to a continually more constricting taxation, far in excess even of that to which we were
forced to submit during the years of the second
World War. It is thus to be noted that, though
income tax has occasionally been imposed as a
means of relieving impoverished groups, the really
serious impositions have been due to the commit-
ments of Washington to civil or foreign wars
or to its conviction of the imminence of a foreign
one.

But before going on to examine the situation in
which we now find ourselves in the midst of the
"cold war" with Russia, let us see where one self-
employed writer of extremely irregular income has
been left, under the present tax laws, by the recent
high tide of taxation. Let us set aside for the moment the penalties and interest on my past arrears.
Let us even set aside the exaction—intolerable in
the case of a writer if not also for everyone else—

that one is made to pay in advance every quarter for money one has not yet earned and to submit to being penalized at the rate of 6% if one falls short beyond a certain amount of guessing correctly one's not yet earned future earnings. In the years 1959 and 1960, I was liable for income tax of, respectively, almost $17,000 and almost $14,000. I had been making far more money during these two years than I had ever made before in my life or am ever likely to make again. Besides a small regular income from a trust fund left by my mother, which brings in about $8,500 a year, I had had a year's lectureship at Harvard for which—incapable as I am of lecturing —I was permitted to present to my class the substance of a book I was writing on the literature of the American Civil War; I had contributed to the *New Yorker* a series of articles on the Iroquois Indians, and had had an advance from a publisher for a book incorporating these articles; and I had been paid for an option on the film rights of my *Memoirs of Hecate County*. The chapters on the Civil War had behind them some twelve years of intermittent work; the articles on the Indians, two; and the writing of the novel, as I have said above, had extended over six years. Now, my income, aside from the trust fund I have mentioned, is entirely derived from my earnings. I have never made any investments, and have indeed had small opportunity to do so. But how much more fortunate I should be if I had may be seen from the following scales of differences, drawn up, says Mr. Harold H. Martin, a writer in the *Saturday Evening Post*, by the Internal Revenue Service: "A taxpayer with a wife and two children, with $7,000 in income derived exclusively from wages or salary, would pay a tax of $780. A taxpayer in similar circumstances, with $7000 in income derived from dividends, would pay $609.60. A taxpayer with $7,000 received from the sale of securities giving him a long-term capital gain would pay a tax of $155. A taxpayer whose $7000 came from interest on state or municipal securities would pay no tax at all." If, better still, I had been an owner of oil wells, and had asserted that my wells were exhausted, I could have claimed for what is technically called "depletion" a tax deduction of 27½% of my gross income. But nobody could be more depleted than a writer very frequently is when he has just made the effort of finishing a book upon which he has been working for years. He may find that it is many months before he can get started again on any considerable project. (James Reston has already made this point, and has suggested that a pretty woman who has been worn out with bearing children or a prizefighter who has taken punishment might also claim deduction for depletion.) But a writer is not entitled to this kind of deduction, nor is he in a posi-

tion to resort to the large-scale juggling devices
exploited by millionaires. He cannot, for example,
take over a money-losing winter resort, dissolve it
as a corporation, and deduct its current expenses, as
long as it continues to lose, from his own personal
tax; then reinstate it as a corporation from the moment it begins making money and get the benefit
of the tax on corporations, which has a ceiling of
52%, instead of the ceiling of 91% on private incomes. A writer may spend years on a book, getting
along on a very small income, and perhaps accumu-
lating debts, and then when the book is published—
if it turns out to be a success—he may find himself
in a high enough bracket so that a third of the
royalties he earns is taken away by the federal
government. It is true that the Internal Revenue
Code provides for what is called a "stretchback" for
this kind of "bunched income"; but this arrangement is still unjust. For if the author is to be in a
position to take advantage of this, it is stipulated that
his work on the book or the play must have occupied
at least twenty-four months and that 80% of its
total earnings must accrue in the taxable year, in
previous years and in twelve months from the end of
the taxable year—though of course the 80% may
overlap a further year and though a book or a play
may do nothing at first but then come to life later
in a film or a paperback. Furthermore, this restricts

the stretchback period to only three years, though
the period of preparation may have taken a good
deal longer—while inventors, in similar situations,
are given a leeway of five, and lawyers, accountants
and other professionals are allowed to spread back
their eventual earnings over as many years as their
long-term services may have taken them to perform.
It has, therefore, been proposed by the Authors
Guild that a five-year system of averaging be
adopted, by which earnings in excess of the average
of the four preceding years may be divided among
those years in such a way that the income for each
shall fall into a lower bracket and the writer may not
be obliged to pay in a higher bracket for the whole
amount earned in the current year. This proposal
has been recommended by the President as an item
of his tax-cutting program, and, at the time of
writing, it has been approved by the House Ways
and Means Committee.*

This reform would, of course, do nothing to alleviate the state taxes, which are piled on the federal
ones and which in my case, during my years of
delinquency, amounted, with penalties and interest,

---

* The writer can also resort to the device of having a
"ceiling clause" included in his contract with his publisher,
according to which the annual payment of royalties may not
exceed a certain sum, but this has to be assayed in advance,
and there is often no way of his knowing even approximately
how much he will make.

to over $10,000. And of course, in addition to these, I must pay a property tax in Massachusetts, a property tax in New York and two other New York taxes, one for schools and one for roads.

Bureaucratic Theology: The Tax Jungle

In the course of my dealings with the IRS, I did not expect comprehension of the peculiar conditions of a writer's work. I doubt whether the men I encountered had ever had to consider such a case before, and I imagine that—having constantly to struggle with offenders who were trying to cover themselves, and inventing ingenious excuses—they did not necessarily believe what I said. But I did at the beginning assume that I was up against an official agency which, guided by definite statutes, would be able to proceed with precision. I was gradually brought to the conclusion that these laws were more or less of a muddle, that, continually becoming more complicated in order to make distinctions between different kinds of income accruing under different conditions, continually being readapted to cope with some special situation and then being found to lend themselves to some new "loophole," that is, abuse, it was becoming harder and harder for even the experts to master them. Not even the best-trained lawyer can apparently find his way through the forests of those gigantic tax books, through the dense print and the obscurely worded sentences of those innumerable exasperating forms which involve supplying endless data about every detail of one's profits and losses, or of one's personal or corporate expenditures. (What was described to me as "a skeleton library" by one of the tax officials comprised nine enormous volumes for 1963 alone, plus another such volume for the basic law and five more for "capital changes.") The question of what ought to be taxed and how much and which deductions ought to be allowed has reached a point of fine-spun complexity that—working in terms of a different set of values—recalls the far-fetched distinctions of medieval theology. You come to feel that there must be somewhere, in the midst of all this pedantry, busy minds that are amusing themselves with gratuitous paradoxes of reasoning. One of my favorites among these paradoxes is the situation in which "A owns a house, rents it for $2,000 a year, while B owns a house which could be rented for $2,000 a year, but which he chooses to use for his own dwelling. Accountants credit A with a $2,000 income, and B with none. Economists argue that B has obtained benefits from living in his house which exactly balance the $2,000 rent A received from his; B has received a 'real' income exactly equivalent to A's monetary income."* The $2,000 that B does not receive is known, technically but beautifully, as "psychic income." One of the most richly diverting departments, however, is that of deductible expenses. A choice selection of the problems raised here is provided in an article in *Time* magazine on the Internal Revenue Service. "The IRS ruled," says *Time*, "that a Hollywood actress could deduct the cost of her expensive wardrobe on the ground that a movie star is required to look well-dressed; but [that] she could not deduct the cost of undergarments because the public did not see them. . . . The court has permitted a taxpayer to deduct the cost of clarinet lessons for a child whose orthodontist recommended them, and a psychiatric patient got away with deducting automobile expenses because his psychiatrist prescribed driving as therapy. But the court disallowed the cost of dancing lessons for a surgery patient, although a doctor recommended dancing for post-operative therapy." The writer might have added the authentic case of the man in a state of neurotic depression whose doctor advised

* *American Public Finance* by William J. Schultz and C. Lowell Harris (Prentice-Hall), p. 562. An excellent book: not a taxpayer's guide but an historical and critical work.

sexual intercourse and who then tried to get a deduction for the money he had spent on call girls, presenting their receipted bills. This gave the authorities some pause, and he almost succeeded in convincing them. The line is drawn very fine, and it takes an acute mind to know exactly where to draw it. Strange principles of value are involved that are quite alien to our ordinary thinking. "A taxpayer," continues the writer in *Time*, "is permitted to deduct educational expenses if they enable him to keep his job, but not if they enable him to get a better job. A specialist in internal medicine, for example, was allowed to deduct the cost of psychoanalysis (he said it would help him to be a better internist), but a psychiatrist was not allowed to do so since analysis might help him become a psychoanaylst—and thereby make more money." An attempt is being made at the present time to impose more severe restrictions on what are known as "business expenses," with a view to cutting down on expensive lunches and lavish entertainment for other business men from out of town. But how does a writer come out on this? I find that it is difficult, at my time of life, to think of anything that I do or anywhere that I go which could not be called a business expense: the books I buy, the libraries I visit, my travel to foreign countries, a good deal of my entertaining, which keeps me in touch with the literary and learned world. What business has the government to demand of me that I itemize and justify all this? What right has the government to say which expenses are and which are not "legitimate"? This is the real realm of "psychic value," with which no government can really deal. It is an insufferable impertinence of the federal government to ask why I have entertained my guests or why I have chosen to travel—to say nothing of how many times I have been married, whom I have voted for and whether or not I buy my dog a bed.*

Aside from the question, to which I shall come, of what our taxpayer's money is used for, there is obviously something wrong with a society which is

* The IRS, with its characteristic volatility, seems now to have reversed this policy. Since the above was written, the *Times* of June 24 has carried a report from Washington to the effect that the code for business men is to be liberalized, with an astonishing generosity, to the extent that "the cost of food and beverages in quiet surroundings, conducive to business discussion," is now to be tax-deductible even if business is not discussed. This keeps them out of the night clubs, since the surroundings are supposed to be quiet, but they don't actually have to talk about business. If I were only a business man, this would cover all my entertaining. Or am I a business man? What is the government's ruling? And the authorities will go even further. The business man, "in some circumstances, will be able to deduct a larger percentage of country club dues and the costs of maintaining a yacht or hunting lodge." I do not sail or hunt or belong to a country club, but why shouldn't I deduct the expenses of the clubs to which I do belong, to which I often invite writers and scholars, though we do not necessarily talk shop, as the IRS has decreed that we don't necessarily have to? The surroundings are always quiet.

subjecting its citizens to this. And it is not merely the citizens in the professional brackets who have most cause to complain about it. My lawyer, on one occasion, had evidently tried to persuade a Utica official that the Internal Revenue Service ought to show consideration to a distinguished man. The answer was that I should be treated "like any ordinary man on Water Street"—not one of the most prosperous parts of Utica. The less well-off people are bullied and nagged as much as the professional ones, and I am protesting on their behalf, too. Both the poor and the professional groups are much easier to get at than the very rich, with their experts in financial sleight-of-hand. In the village where I spend my summers, my neighbors are continually being prodded and made to feel insecure by the pressure of the IRS. One of them has had to sell his car and give up his telephone and will perhaps remain in debt to the government all the rest of his life. Another, a young lumber-truck driver, who frequently stops off on his long all-night trips for snacks and coffee to keep him from going to sleep has been ordered by the tax office, which cannot imagine why he should visit the roadside diners so many times in a night, to submit to them an explanation for his spending so much on meals and to provide it with evidence that his money has been spent for the purposes indicated. (If, as happens, a truck driver goes to sleep and over-

turns the truck, he may be seriously injured and then
fined by the company.) An expert in educational
guidance has been summoned to present receipts
for his small contributions to church work and for
the bi-monthly visits of his invalid wife to a doctor in
a neighboring town. A young wife, who has a job in
a mill and has been leaving her two children with
her sister-in-law, has learned that it is not admissible
to deduct expenses for baby-sitting if you and
your husband's joint income is over $4,500 a year.
A young woman who works in a pharmacy is
subjected to an $11 withholding on her $60 a
week. The merchants have to put down as assets the
credit to customers which they cannot collect; and
if a storekeeper is found delinquent, the federal
agents can go into his store and take the money out
of his cash register, just as they went into my publisher's office and ordered him to hand over my
royalties. The 60,000 officials who are appointed to
check on us taxpayers are checked on, themselves,
it seems, by another group of agents set to watch
them. And supplementing these officials—since private citizens are paid by the IRS to report on other
people's delinquencies, and their names of course
are never revealed—there is a whole host of amateur
investigators, estimated as of 1961 at a hundred
thousand, seven hundred and six of whom earned
in that year $548,914 by betraying their relations and

acquaintances and bringing in twelve million dollars
of which the government might not otherwise have
known. Does this kind of spying and delation differ
much in its incitement to treachery from that which
is encouraged in the Soviet Union? We have, it seems,
in the United States, been offering attractive rewards
for the action of close associates and married people
who inform against one another from motives of
spite or gain. This practice has been proved to be so
lucrative that it is said to have been recently increasing.*

The collection of taxes and the avoidance of
taxes have now become national industries. There
has grown up as opposite numbers of these 60,000
tax officials a corps of 80,000 lawyers who are occupied exclusively with taxes, and there are also
the accountants who work with them, and the
thousands of other lawyers whose practice is also
more or less in tax matters. A professor at Chicago
Law School tells me that he has estimated that half
of the top 10% of the school's graduating class has
been, during the last ten years, devoting at least half
its working time to tax cases. The government lays
upon us the obligation not merely to hand over to
it, above a very moderate bracket, a third or more of
what we make, but also, in addition, if we have not

* An article by Gerald Krefetz in the New York *Times*
Magazine Section of April, 1962.

the time or the aptitude to attend to such matters
ourselves, to pay out considerable sums to experts in
law and accounting, who try to circumvent its
unmanageable statutes and to save for us, by pleas
and excuses, as large a share as possible of that income of which our national propaganda assumes
that we are freely disposing in our enjoyment of "the
American way of life." The atmosphere of the
tax-ridden United States is reminiscent of the Prohibition era, except that it is a good deal grimmer.
Among the population in general, these tax laws are
felt, at the least, as a constraining and menacing em-
barrassment which our legislators have got on the
books we do not know exactly how and with which
we are less and less able to contend at the same time
that we are less and less prepared to conform. The
day I was haled into court, the judge was knocking
off the cases of a series of income tax culprits as if
they were so many bootleggers. The *New York
Times* of August 12 announces that "the fiscal year
1963 saw an increase of more than 10% in convictions
of income tax violators."

The Point of View of a Former Socialist

It may perhaps be wondered why a former Leftist, who in 1932, at the time of the great depression, when the Communist Party was legal, voted for the Communist candidates in the presidential election and who voted for Norman Thomas thereafter up to the time when he ceased to run, should be making so much fuss about state control. Had I not, in voting for socialism, been voting for the state control of industry? Had I not at that time been in favor of expropriating the profits of the rich and expending them for the welfare of the many? Well, I must confess with compunction that I was naïve enough at thirty-one to take seriously Lenin's prediction in his pamphlet *State and Revolution*, written in 1917 on the eve of his return to Russia, that the clerical work of a socialist government could easily be attended to in the spare time of ordinary citizens who were otherwise occupied with higher things, and that the State, under the new regime, no longer needed by a governing class, would inevitably "wither away" and cease to harass the individual, who would be eager by that time to coöperate in promoting the general harmony of a frictionless because classless society—though the critics of Saint-Simon and the other early nineteenth-century communists had predicted the opposite result: the growth of a huge bureaucracy and the eventual omnipotence of the State. And it was possible also in the days when the Third International seemed to function as a working-class organization to imagine that it might ultimately succeed in rescuing labor from exploitation and humanity from its horrible wars. It was assumed that the working class could maintain an international solidarity and that it did not want horrible wars. But both these assumptions were incorrect. The "working class," as it was then conceived by the persons of whatever origins who acted on these suppositions, has to be recognized today as a Marxist fiction. In the Soviet Union, for example, you no longer have the "workers and peasants" who composed the official soviets (councils): you have partially educated persons exploited by a class of officials in the interests of an intense Russian nationalism and admitted to the official ranks only if they are ready to subscribe to the Russian official dogmas; and there is hardly any longer in the United States any such thing as the old-fashioned farmer who finds himself sold up by the bankers, or the old-fashioned sweated factory worker. Both of these are now dependent on bureaucracies to whom they may appeal or protest: the former on the Department of Agriculture, the second on the labor unions. And as for the group of "mechanics," hardly distinguishable from that of "engineers," both of whom are called in Russia "technicians," they are very far from having developed, as Thornton Veblen and others once thought they might, any inclination to revolution, nor are they interested in preventing war. There are so many of them employed in the industries that are preparing us for a war of annihilation that nothing could dismay them more than the prospect of having these industries shut down. The workers with their hands in the Soviet Union as well as those in the United States now have as their principal aim what would once have been called middle-class comfort, and in societies which pretend to be governed by opposite "ideologies," they have both become extremely docile.

Lenin lived long enough, though he survived the Bolshevik revolution only a little longer than seven years, to be alarmed and disgusted by the growth of bureaucracy and to warn his party against it. The American socialists never dreamed of the danger of bureaucratic control. They were idealists, rather innocent and backward from the European point of view, full of old-fashioned brotherly "democracy," who were thinking in terms of constitutional methods by which socialists would be voted into office in a United States which, even with socialism, would continue to be more loosely united than our present-day centralized government, which is becoming more and more rigid because more and more mechanized (the Internal Revenue Service is now already using computers to indicate automatically any sudden rise or fall of income). One cannot really indicate this difference by assuming that there is anything in common between, on the one hand, the programs of the old American socialists and, on the other, the measures of nationalization, of intervention in industrial disputes and of the granting of government subsidies which have actually been put into practice in the course of the New Deal and of subsequent administrations. Norman Thomas and the early Max Eastman as well as Eugene Debs were imagining an extension of democracy which would get the big "capitalist" off the "wage-slave's" neck and restore the American community to the realization of something like Walt Whitman's vision of a robust fraternal race exploring and cultivating and building and enjoying the country's resources. Among presidents, Franklin Roosevelt in his feudal Hudson River way had something of this generous spirit; President Kennedy, as an Irishman and a

Catholic, has something of this magnanimity, too. But our gigantic bureaucracies in Washington have shown as little of this once much-advertized American spirit as any government of a Communist state. One can as little imagine a member of either saying with Eugene Debs, "So long as there is a soul in prison I am not free" as the prosecutor who carried out Stalin's orders to have millions of Soviet citizens executed, the judge who sentenced the Rosenbergs to execution and Morton Sobell, on very slender evidence, to thirty years in Alcatraz or the FBI officials who, on evidence equally dubious, constructed the case against Alger Hiss. We and the Soviet Union, in spite of our competitive boasts and our nasty recriminations, are both at this point well advanced in what used to be called invidiously "State Socialism" in order to distinguish it from a socialism which was intended to be more beneficent, which would somehow free everyone from bondage and give everyone enough to eat. The "State" in both cases consists of a kind of mechanical organism of interlocking official departments, with a nominal leader at the nominal top who is taxed one would think almost beyond endurance by the effort to keep his hand on the complicated, ill-coördinated and often refractory controls.

But we taxpayers are putting up the costs, to the

tune of a hundred billion dollars, of two-thirds of these machines' expenses. Let us consider for what purposes they are using this money which we are giving them so submissively and why they think they require so much.

What Our Money Is Going For

A very large proportion of the money that was raised by the government during Roosevelt's first two administrations was devoted to measures, whether well- or ill-advised, which were intended to alleviate the miseries of poverty and unemployment resulting from the great depression: the Agricultural Adjustment Act, the National Recovery Administration, the Public Works Administration, the Tennessee Valley Authority, the Social Security Act, the Works Progress Administration, etc. These all involved centralized government control, and they were usually applauded by the "liberals" and denounced by the champions of old-fashioned laissez-faire, who presently began talking about "creeping socialism." But the subsequent development of this centralized control has been something not foreseen by the liberals and, though no longer directed mainly to social ends, has perhaps proved even more uncomfortable for what Roosevelt called the "economic Bourbons."

What our money is at present being spent for is presented in a very frank way by the issue for the fiscal year ending July 1, 1964, of the elegantly printed brochure called *The Budget in Brief*, put out yearly by the Bureau of the Budget. This begins with the following statement: "The Nation faces unprecedented challenges at home, abroad, and in outer space. . . . In 1964, the Federal Government will continue to build a defensive and retaliatory power designed to deter aggression. At the same time, it will seek to strengthen the foundations of freedom around the world; to serve a wide range of vital and ever-changing domestic needs; to press forward with the Nation's response to the scientific challenge of the vast and mysterious frontier of space; and to support all of these efforts by promoting a strong and growing economy." There follows a boxed quotation from President Kennedy's message on the budget, pointing out that "it is of importance to assure more jobs for an ever growing labor force, if we are to achieve higher standards of living, and if we are to continue to provide the leadership required of us in the free world community."

But it will be seen that the emphasis here is laid mainly on defense and retaliation, giving financial support to other countries and sending missiles and rockets into outer space. Even supplying more jobs is not required merely for the purpose of achieving a higher standard of living for the citizens of the United States but also, and perhaps more importantly, in order to equip the United States for the leadership of "the free world community" (a conception to be examined later). The exposition of the program continues:

"The Federal Government's final responsibility is to help safeguard the peace and security of the free world. This is our largest category of expenditures. Complementing the defense effort, international programs support the cause of freedom in many ways.

"We have mounted an accelerated effort to explore space, an effort which will give top priority to a manned landing on the moon during this decade.

"Expenditures devoted to national security needs, to space programs, and to paying for the continuing costs of past wars amount to 79% of the administrative budget. . . ."

We now come to education, which gets a kind of incidental mention in a sentence that includes also "community development, transportation and man power." Now, in view of our underpaid teachers who are obliged to go on strike for a raise and our illiterate city children who inhabit a world of gang warfare, unaware that any larger world exists, it is obvious that education is the most pressing need of the United States; yet the President has been having great difficulty in getting his education bills put through, and the fact that, in this budget statement, the question of education is assigned to a very subordinate place while a "manned landing on the moon" is played up and given "top priority" suggests that our House and Senate, themselves often only semi-literate, may find this spectacular exploit more attractive than better facilities for education. Is the public who reads the headlines as stupid as this makes it out? I am afraid that a good deal of it probably is. An article by Warren Weaver in the *Saturday Review* (August 4, 1962) has examined this overpowering absurdity—the idea that a trip to the moon is a crying national need—without, so far as I know, making any impression on anyone with influence. Mr. Weaver points out that it has been forecast that to "put a man on the moon" may cost thirty billion dollars. For the sum of thirty billion dollars, we could give, he says, "a 10% raise in salary to every teacher in the United States, from kindergarten through universities, in both public and private institutions (about $9.8 billion); give $10,000,000 each to two hundred of the best smaller

colleges ($2 billion); finance seven-year fellow-
ships (freshmen through Ph.D.) at $4,000 per per-
son per year for 50,000 new scientists and engineers
($1.4 billion); contribute $200 million each toward
the creation of ten new medical schools ($2 billion);
build and largely endow complete universities, with
medical, engineering and agricultural faculties for all
fifty-three of the nations which have been added to
the United Nations since its original founding ($13.2
billion); create three more permanent Rockefeller
Foundations ($1.5 billion); and still have $100 million left over to popularize science." What is this
breakneck competition between us and the Soviet
Union for planting a flag on the moon and for the
navigation of space, when our big cities are dark
unhealthy horrors, so crowded, impeded and chaotic
that they have hardly the dignity of the anthills to
which they used to be compared, and when our
mountains and countrysides are partly inhabited by
human mammals who do not really differ much in
intelligence from the vermin with which they contend? The answer is: this space competition has
become an international sport—the interests of
science by themselves could never have stimulated
the government to the point of this tremendous
financing—of which the initial impetus is like that
of the Olympic games. I do not mean to be contemptuous of games. The physical powers of

humanity are as important as their intellectual ones; and in the achievements of spacemen and pilots the two are impressively combined. Even someone who must sit for many hours a day only moving a pencil with his wrist or lying in an easy chair while his eyes run through the lines of a book can understand the joy of soaring far above our little limited earth and of destroying one's earthbound brothers by the click that releases a bomb. An American woman married to an Austrian writer who lived through the last war near Munich has told me of the nonchalance of an American or British bomber who amused himself by circling above the countryside and knocking off the farmers' cattle as well as sometimes the farmers and their families. The Germans had the time of their lives playing God to Coventry and London, and the British and Americans had the satisfaction of playing the winning God when they needlessly laid Dresden waste, incinerating and blowing up more people than were killed by the Americans in Hiroshima. It is easy to understand the exhilaration and pride which the flyers derive from all this. Human life since Stalin and the Nazis has been something that few people in the East or the West any longer care much about. The only serious qualms of most of us who make a habit of reading the papers are inspired by a fear for our own skins; and those who do not read the papers—they are many, and there are not many papers which convey any real information—seem hardly to have begun worrying about this.

But before going on to the question of war, I want to put in my own objection, of a special occupational kind, to the cost of a trip to the moon.

What About American Literature?

I understand that a good deal of the money appropriated for scientific research is actually spent through the universities, in which studies and projects are subsidized and huge atomic instruments installed at the expense of the federal government. This, it seems, is not regarded by these institutions as entirely a benefaction. The government is determined to dictate what these agencies and instruments shall be used for, and the colleges sometimes rebel. But at least it cannot be said that the government is doing nothing for science.* What is it doing for literature?

* Karl E. Meyer, in the *New Statesman* of August 9, 1963, makes the following statement: "A top-level White House report in 1962 found that federally financed research has grown from $100 million annually in the Thirties to $10,000 million a year at present—and that 80 per cent of the work is currently being conducted in various non-governmental institutions."

The Library of Congress, and its jobs that are sometimes given to authors, the excellent White House dinners to which authors are sometimes asked, the exemption from income tax of the university presses, which are thus allowed easier conditions for publishing valuable books from which they can expect no profit. But does the government do anything else to encourage the national literature? So far as I know, nothing.*

I have for years—since sometime during World War II—been attempting to arouse an interest on the part of some publishing house or other organization in bringing out a series of complete editions of the principal American classics in convenient form and at a moderate price. It is absurd that our American prose writers who are today most studied and written about should not have been made available in well-edited texts. The sole collected edition of Melville was published in England in the twenties and has long been out of print; and there is not and has never been of Parkman or Henry Adams or Henry or William James any complete collected edition at all. The only serious effort, on any large scale, to do justice to our most valued writers has been the publication by Houghton, Mifflin of such New Englanders as Thoreau, Hawthorne and Emer-

---

* Since this was first written, three American writers have been awarded "Freedom Medals."

son, and these editions, too, are now out of print. The old out-of-print edition of Cooper contains only his novels, and not even all of these (though, to be sure, a well-managed selection would be preferable to Cooper complete). There has never been a scholarly edition of Poe which even aimed at comprehensiveness and accuracy except that made by James A. Harrison of the University of Virginia, and this has also long been out of print. A collected edition of Howells was begun during his lifetime but has never been completed. There was a collected Stephen Crane, published expensively in the twenties by Knopf, but this is only to be found in large libraries. As for the writers of less importance, a volume of whose selected best work should be also put in circulation—John DeForest, Henry Fuller, Harold Frederic and the poets and chroniclers and essayists and writers of travels and memoirs who, though not of the very first rank, are of special interest to anyone who is interested in our history and culture—they have sometimes been reprinted lately in a more or less hit-or-miss fashion but nothing systematic and discriminating has ever been done about them.

The kind of thing I should like to see available is a series like the French Éditions de la Pléiade, which has included so many of the French classics, ancient and modern, in attractively produced and admirably printed thin-paper volumes, ranging from eight to fifteen hundred pages. These volumes, published by Gallimard, have evidently proved commercially successful, for they are prominently on display in every book store in Paris and everywhere that French books are sold. In Italy, Mondadori has been publishing the Italian classics in a very similar format, though not on the same scale. But Benedetto Croce persuaded another Italian publisher, Laterza, to bring out the series called *Scrittori d'Italia* as well as a philosophical series, the former of which includes such not easily available works as Sarpi's histories and the macaronic poets. In England, the Oxford Press has published the English poets and a good deal of English prose in cheap and well-edited volumes. The Soviet government has been publishing the best editions that have ever existed (though with occasional ridiculous omissions at the behest of the political censorship) of the Russian nineteenth-century classics. Only in the United States, at a time when our literature, both here and abroad, has been receiving more attention than ever before, has this national literature never really, in any satisfactory way, been put into circulation. There has been a certain amount of reprinting in the John Harvard Library, published by the Harvard University Press, and in the various paperback series, but this has been haphazard and scrappy.

It is hard to see how such a project could be car-

ried out, even through the agency of one of the
foundations, except with the assistance of the government. It has been estimated that the program could
be started with an investment of not much more than
$500,000 for the first three years. This assumes that
ten new volumes would be published every year,
each consisting of an average of 1200 pages and sell-
ing for a retail price of $12. If a minimum of 3000
copies of each volume were sold during the first year
and 500 in each of several years thereafter, it has
been calculated that the enterprise should become
self-sustaining in five or six years. But what would
be the chances of getting half a million dollars for
this purpose when "the nation" needs so many bil-
lions to respond to "the scientific challenge of the
vast and mysterious frontier of space"? What are
the chances of a small contribution to making accessible the work of those writers who have accepted
the challenge of the vast and mysterious frontier of
non-space-exploring human experience? It is difficult
to imagine such an item's receiving the slightest
notice in the preamble of *The Budget in Brief*. Yet
the proposal has been cordially welcomed by most
of the principal scholars who have been teaching
and writing or otherwise occupying themselves with
American literature: W. H. Auden, Jacques Barzun,
Maurice Bewley, R. P. Blackmur, Van Wyck
Brooks, Alfred Kazin, Perry Miller, Norman Holmes

Pearson, John Crowe Ransom, Allen Tate, Lionel Trilling, Mark Van Doren and Robert Penn Warren; and it has even been recommended—not to Congress but to whom it may concern—in a letter from President Kennedy.

It may be mentioned in this connection that the French government has now for decades been contributing to the publication of works of French literature and history. I am informed by M. André Malraux, the French Minister of Cultural Affairs, that the French government at the present time, through a Caisse Nationale des Lettres, is partly subsidizing new editions of the complete works of Ernest Renan, Gérard de Nerval and Paul Verlaine, the correspondence of Balzac and Villiers de l'Isle Adam, critical editions of Charles Nodier and Madame de Staël, learned works such as *L'Histoire des Monuments détruits de l'Art français*, bilingual editions and translations of such foreign writers as Goethe and Kleist, and a number of other works. I was rather surprised to learn that a new edition of *Les Stances* of Jean Moréas had been subsidized. Moréas may be taken as a kind of equivalent of some of the lesser Americans mentioned above. This book of his is a landmark of the Parnassian school of poetry, and is needed by students of French literature, but in 1959 only 309 copies were sold; in 1960, 52; and in 1961, 24. In view of this falling off, the publisher,

the *Mercure de France,* successfully applied to the
government for aid in bringing out a new printing.
Among other projects subsidized by the government
are new critical editions of Pascal, and of the complete correspondence of Voltaire, Chateaubriand and
Flaubert. And subsidies have also been granted to a
number of contemporary writers to entable them to
carry out their work. Among these have been Blaise
Cendrars, Louis Guilloux, Pierre-Jean Jouve and
François Ponge.

But the French are only just beginning to enjoy
the intoxication of spending the national income for
nuclear weapons, and if they go on to indulge themselves freely, Jean Moréas may have to be dropped,
if not also Voltaire, Chateaubriand and all the rest.

How Can We Account for Ourselves?

Our own spree of spending on nuclear weapons—
that is, our government's spree—and the public's indifference to it is one of the most remarkable phe-
nomena—if it does not prove to be one of the last—in
the history of Western civilization. We inaugurated
atomic warfare in 1945, when we wiped out the two

Japanese towns—gratuitously, and in disregard of an officially appointed committee which had predicted that this would make us unpopular and recommended a non-lethal demonstration which would convince the Japanese of the effectiveness of our weapons. It has been known for a long time now that, before the Hiroshima attack, Stalin had been notified by the Japanese of their willingness to negotiate peace, but it had always been said that Stalin, in a desire to prolong the conflict long enough to give the Russians a chance to participate in the defeat of Japan, had concealed this news from President Truman. It now appears, however, that Truman was fully informed. A conversation at Potsdam between Stalin and Truman was recorded by Charles Bohlen, who has revealed, in a recent statement, that the President would not take this peace feeler seriously, declaring that he could not trust the Japanese. When the offer was repeated ten days later, he still declined to talk terms and immediately had the bomb dropped. It has also been revealed, in an article in *Look* magazine of August 13,* that a considerable body of scientific opinion was opposed to the unannounced use of the bomb. General George C.

* This article, by Fletcher Knebel and Charles W. Bailey, is based on new material unearthed from the official files. The authors have had these facts for two years but permission to make them public has only just been given by the State Department.

Marshall wrote, "We must offset by . . . warning methods the opprobrium which might follow from an ill-considered employment of such force." James B. Conant foresaw "super-super bombs" delivered by guided missiles and urged Secretary of War Stimson to first demonstrate "Little Boy" and "Fat Man," as the bombs were affectionately known, before unloading them on the Japanese. (On Conant, however, see p. 96.) An atomic productions man named O. C. Brewster wrote to President Truman: "This thing must not be permitted to exist upon earth. We must not be the most hated and feared people on earth, however good our intent may be. So long as the threat against Germany existed, we had to proceed with all speed to accomplish this end. With the threat of Germany removed, we must stop this project." Leo Szilard and seventy of his colleagues petitioned Truman to consider the "moral responsibilities" involved in the use of the bomb and not to use it unless terms of surrender had been definitely rejected by the Japanese. But this petition and others were not allowed to reach the President. They were side-tracked by Major General Leslie R. Groves, the Army engineer who built the Pentagon, who put through the project of constructing the bomb and who was firmly in favor of dropping it.

President Truman, Major General Groves is

quoted in this article as saying, "was like a little boy on a toboggan," who never had a real chance to say yes. But how can we explain the eagerness of Major General Groves and others to annihilate these Japanese cities when there was no necessity for doing so, regardless of the obvious danger of terrifying and antagonizing the rest of the world? The fact that the Japanese had fought us in the fiercest way and savagely tortured our soldiers ought to have been irrelevant for a nation which boasted itself in the advance guard of civilization. How, then, did we champions of freedom, with our mission to protect the world, come to spend enormous sums of money on enthusiastically developing these weapons? This can only, I believe, be explained by an irrepressible combination, on our part, of the instinctive impulsion to power, which in a state implies the power to crush, and the technological passion which is undoubtedly, among the workings of the human creative, or inventive, genius, the predominant one of the age. We claimed, of course, that we were defending ourselves against the Russians. But why did we have to fear them? We had no border in common with them. It was absurd to imagine that they wanted to invade us. They had already quite enough to think about with their recalcitrant captive nations in Europe. As for the Communist Party in the United States, it was so tiny that it would have been absurd to take it seriously as a subversive influence, and its membership, it seems, is now largely composed of FBI agents. There was, to be sure, the old business man's nightmare of being robbed of his profits by the Socialist State (which, ironically, is now being done on the pretext of protecting him against socialism); and this does partly account for our fear of the Soviets. There is also the periodical American panic, which dates from the Revolution, at the thought of being dominated by a foreign power. And then there are commercial interests: oil in Iran, rubber in Vietnam, sugar plantations in Cuba, etc. All this may be enough, I suppose, to produce the national nightmare of a United States first surrounded—Cuba, Canada, South America—by the insidious Soviet forces, then annexed by a Communist power and our inhabitants reduced to the status of slave labor. In any case, many Americans were shaken by a horrible shudder when Khrushchyov, in one of his speeches for home consumption, predicted that Communism would "bury" us—perhaps because we were already half-buried by income tax extortions, official bamboozlement and suppression of civil rights.

Yet the whole world had reason to shudder when we detonated the first atomic bombs. The Soviets soon came to be as scared of us as we have come to be of them. It was not without plausibility that they began to denounce us as "warmongers"—since we

proceeded from the "nominal atomic bomb" that
obliterated Hiroshima and disintegrated its inhabitants by radioactivity to a hydrogen bomb of twenty
megatons that could devastate Moscow at a single
blast; and there has been talk of a cobalt bomb which,
from the point of view of radiation casualties as distinguished from burning and blasting, would be
found even more effective. Our government has also
been working on a project for a neutron bomb which
would have the immense advantage of destroying the
human beings while leaving the buildings intact.
What could be neater than this? We incinerate the
people and take over the plant. That, as a result of
this radioactivity, our race may degenerate later,
cannot be taken into consideration in our contest
with the Soviet Union to show ourselves techno-
logically top man. Now, the Russians, on their side,
have been genuinely alarmed ever since their Revolution—much as we were after ours in regard to
England and France—lest the "capitalist" world
should gang up on them and suppress their "Marxist-
Leninist" state; and if the United States was piling up
megaton bombs after Germany had been crushed and
divided, what else could they have in mind? Had not
loud American voices declared war to the death on
the Communist world? Were we not encircling this
world by air bases in England, Spain, Turkey and
Japan? Were we not, with this end in view, sending

troops to assure our ascendancy over South Korea, Laos and Vietnam? The Russians began to race us, and the race ran to long-distance missiles. We can launch these now from specially constructed and very expensive submarines, and the Soviets now assert that they can pulverize our cities without ever leaving Russia. At one point, we were wailing about a "missile gap" between our resources and the Russians' in as ludicrously juvenile a way—and our opponents sounded equally juvenile—as if we were a freshwater college which had lost the big game of the season and was in danger of forfeiting its championship. When the stakes in games become so serious—when everybody's life is at stake—they ought not to be played at all, and the taxpayers should not support them.

But the taxpayers do support them, and that is why we cannot halt these activities. How much do the taxpayers know about the objects that their money is going for? About nuclear weapons, something. But they confuse nuclear weapons with sputniks and putting a man on the moon, as they are encouraged to do—see *The Budget in Brief*—by being told that the mastery of space is important for the world supremacy, the real Big League championship, at which we are supposed to be aiming.

The truth is that this triumph of technology has left most of us far behind. For the ordinary person who is not a technician, the terms in which he can imagine the situation are likely to be the familiar terms of sport. The mechanic and the engineer, the pilot and the Polaris crew are the heroes for our side of a great international sport, and they are so much a part of the processes which they are fascinated and proud to be mastering that they do not give themselves any leeway to think about the ends these serve. The bureaucrats who formulate and administer the projects that the technicians are carrying out are also extremely preoccupied—in this case with their bureaucratic careers, and, so concentrating, they cannot afford to question. If one of the atomic physicists who were involved in the original manufacture of the bomb makes an attempt, like Leo Szilard, to put the brakes on it and avert its consequences by organizing a lobby for peace, or, like Edward Teller, tries to mitigate its horror by insisting that these consequences will not be so bad as we think, since though millions will of course be incinerated, a certain number will be left alive, this does little to hinder the progress of the technological forces which are directed to works of destruction.

To me, it seems strange that the American public can keep on reading, year after year, the news reports that deal with these matters, and not merely not bring pressure to bear in an outbreak of popular feeling but become so accustomed to reading such reports that they do not seem to be as much alarmed by them as by the news of a mad strangler at large in their neighborhood.

On July 12, 1957, one learned from the New York *Times* that, on account of "economy cuts in the vast Air Force program," the Air Force was "abandoning the Navaho intercontinental guided missile," work on which had begun in 1946, immediately after the war, and upon the development of which had been spent about $500,000,000. It was explained by the Air Force Secretary that "the Navaho should not be considered a loss, but rather a superseded development, from which useful benefits have been derived." How many readers wrote to their senators that they might have preferred to expend for themselves the share they had been made to contribute of this five hundred million dollars? If any did, they made no impression. But it was not merely the ordinary citizen who failed to grasp the situation: that the Administration itself could not really envisage this situation was demonstrated by its vague and irresolute gestures in the direction of providing shelters. It was the State of New York, however, which took the first step in this direction. In the issue of the New York *Times* of July 7, 1959, it was reported on the front page of the *Times* that Governor Rockefeller had given his "full endorsement" to a report which recommended a state law "requiring the construction of thick-walled protective shelters in existing homes and shelters as well as in future homes and buildings," an intensive educational program to warn and instruct citizens, and the "development of a 'special survival kit' of food and other necessities, including a radiation warning device, to enable persons to remain safely in their shelters for at least two weeks in a radioactive area." It was then, however, discovered that the majority leader of the state assembly who had instigated this proposal had an interest in the local company which was in line to supply these shelters. A row was made in Albany. The scandal was glossed over by the Governor, but the shelter legislation was dropped. On May 25, 1961, President Kennedy, in his message to Congress, demanded, in the department of Civil Defense, "triple funds for fall-out shelters, warning measures, stockpiles of food and other needs against nuclear attack." On August 2, it was announced by Secretary of Defense McNamara that the government was taking measures to construct "50,000,000 usable shelter spaces providing a 'Spartan' minimum for one-fourth of the population." This would not mean, he added, "that 50,000,000 lives would be saved, since millions in shelters would die from blast, heat and immediate radiation effects." Now, a statement prepared by eight professors of physics, molecular biology, microbiology and electrical engineering, published in the *Saturday Evening Post* of April 14, 1962, as a reply to an article of Teller's, denies the feasibility of a suggestion made by Teller that the whole urban population of the United States could be crowded, at a few minutes notice, into a shelter system built two hundred feet underground, and asserts that, in the event of a nuclear attack, it is unlikely that anyone would survive. The public, in any case, paid little attention to Secretary McNamara's announcement—though a few constructed amateur shelters, and even equipped themselves with firearms in order to fight off possible neighbors who, having already been exposed to radioactivity and in a condition to communicate it, might attempt to take refuge with them. On June 1, 1962, the Pentagon announced that the first shelters—only twelve of them, housing 1,750 persons—were to be built for the Forest Service at a cost of $300,000. This seemed a modest beginning, but now we read in the *Times* of July 4, 1963—two years after McNamara's announcement—that considerable progress has been made in Manhattan. For example: "In a bare storage room on the 43-story roof of the Waldorf-Astoria, the Government program has stockpiled food and other supplies to keep 7,500 persons alive for two weeks while they wait for outdoor radiation to dissipate . . . the Federal food supply is a biscuit resembling graham crackers in appearance and taste." The Chase Manhattan Bank, on the other hand, has provided its own supplies. It has imported from Norway a foodstuff that is packed in containers the size of a brick and that "comes in banana, chocolate and basic wheat flavors." The Waldorf-Astoria and the bank have drums for water but no water in them. The vice-president of the latter, however, declares that there is available from the tanks, pipes and firelines of the bank enough for two weeks. As I write (July 12, 1963), it is announced that, "The Administration won a major victory for its civil defense program today. It set the stage for a new drive to provide atomic shelters protection for millions of Americans." Though Congress had in the past been reluctant to approve an appropriation for shelters, a sub-committee of the House Armed Services Committee has now been persuaded to authorize, if voted, an expenditure of seventy-five billion dollars. Are these shelters really taken seriously? What are they expected to accomplish? It is evident that the government hardly knows, that it is compromising between skepticism and panic. And yet we have to pay millions for its irresolution and ineptitude.

In the meantime, there had been the tests. We were assured on June 1, 1962, that the Federal Radiation Council had come to the comforting conclusion that "the chances are extremely small that any one person will suffer from fall-out." You may wonder what this means. Read on. "It [the report] estimates, for example, that the chances that an individual in the next generation will suffer a gross physical or mental defect are 1 in 1,000,000." As for persons in the next generation, it was calculated "that in the next seventy years the chances an individual will contract leukemia from fall-out radiation are 1 in 100,000 and 1 in 300,000, for bone cancer. . . . Over the next seventy years, for example . . . a total of 2,700 persons may die from leukemia and bone cancer . . . at an average rate of forty a year. But in comparison, in the same period, a total of 980,000 persons will die from these malignant diseases brought on by other causes. [How does that alleviate the situation of the 2,700 who will be dying of these diseases as the result of an order of the United States Government?] In the next generation of children . . . the fall-out radiation should cause about 110 gross physical or mental defects. This would be in addition to the estimated total of 4,000,000 to 6,000,000 cases of such defects that would be expected normally." Why did Kennedy, when he first became President, not announce that we were going to cease testing? This would have fortified American morale and taken the wind out of the Russians' sails. We both of us had already enough nuclear weapons to disintegrate one another into our constituent atoms. Well, Kennedy is the captain of our team, and he can't afford to let our side down when the boys in the opposite hemisphere are making those big stinks.

On June 26 of this year, a bill was passed by the House for the second largest annual defense appropriation in peacetime in the history of the United States: over forty-seven billion dollars; the largest was last year's: over forty-eight billion. This was followed on June 30, however, by an announcement that "The administration is giving serious consideration to ordering the first substantial cutback in the production of atomic weapons since the United States began building up its nuclear arsenal after World War II. Behind the current study is a belief that the United States, with an arsenal of tens of thousands of atomic weapons, has a sufficient and perhaps an excessive number of nuclear arms to meet its military needs. There also is rising concern in high Administration circles over the multiplying number of warheads that have been assigned to the military forces in the last five years. The major fear is that a continuing profusion would only increase the chances of accidental explosion or unauthorized use of the weapon." It now appeared, from recent statements of the Joint Congressional Committee on Atomic Energy, that a suspicion had arisen in the minds of "many committee members that the production of atomic weapons was coming to be based more on the capabilities of the Atomic Energy Commission to manufacture them than on the actual requirements of the military." But why is it, one is tempted to ask, that we tax-payers and newspaper-readers, who now have impositions to complain of on the part of our own government far heavier and infinitely more dangerous than the American colonists did when they revolted against the Crown—why is it that we citizens of the United States, who established our independence only a century and three quarters ago, have not rebelled against these impositions and refused to provide further funds for a hypothetical war that there was no reason to fear in the first place? What, however, one should really be asking—since we no longer have taxation *without* representation—is why the voters should keep on sending to Congress representatives who are willing to vote for such a monstrous allocation of these funds. The forty-seven billion dollar defense appropriation passed the House, for example, by 410 to 1, and the only man who voted against it explained that he did not disapprove of the purposes of the bill, but merely believed that the amount should be somewhat reduced because "we haven't got the money." Two reasons for this acquiescence are no doubt, as I have already suggested, a failure to grasp what is happening and the appeal of our contest with Russia to the sporting imagination. But before going into the matter further, I want to point out some features of our defense policy which do not have a sporting appeal and of which the general public has hardly become even conscious, both because they have been little publicized and because they are so disagreeable that one has been glad to disregard this publicity. The gigantic mushroom-shaped cloud has a certain heroic grandeur, but there is nothing heroic or grand about chemical and biological weapons.

The Artificial Cholera Epidemic

The first extensive use of chemical weapons occurred during the first World War, when the combatants began with tear gas, which was only an incapacitating nuisance, but soon progressed to toxic gases, which could scarify, asphyxiate and kill. The Hague Convention of 1899 had included a prohibition against "the employment of poison and poisoned weapons," and this had been supplemented by an agreement "to abstain from the use of projectiles the sole object of which is the diffusion of asphyxiating or deleterious gases." The United States ratified the first of these, but refused to ratify the second, explaining through one of its delegates, Admiral Mahan, that every advance in the use of lethal weapons, beginning with firearms, had been denounced as cruel, and that shells with asphyxiating gases could "produce decisive results" and were no worse than anything else. In the Convention of 1907, the subject of gas warfare was dropped, so that everyone felt free to use gas by the time the first World War began. The subject was, however, raised again at the Geneva Conference of 1925. The treaty drawn up at this conference prohibited the use of gas, as "condemned by a concensus of the civilized world," and extended the prohibition to bacteriological warfare. It was signed by forty-two countries, but not by the United States. The treaty was debated for a time in the Senate but then allowed to go to sleep in committee, and eventually, by President Truman, declared to be obsolete.

The United States has, in any case, resorted to gas in its warfare with the Vietnamese, which, according to the New York *Times*, is costing us a million dollars a day, in the interest of imposing a Catholic ruler on a population predominantly and recalcitrantly Buddhist. A report by the Red Cross and Homer Bigart's dispatches in the *Times*—which resulted in his expulsion by the American authorities —make it plain that we are spraying the country

with something which kills vegetation and, it is also
said, cattle. The Pentagon's account of this makes it
sound extremely innocent. We are merely "defoliat-
ing" the bushes and trees in order to be able to see
the Communist guerrillas more clearly, and the chemical preparation used is no more harmful than the
gardener's weed-killer. Yet this spray kills crops as
well as foliage, and so leaves the people to starve.
We have learned, also, from Bigart's dispatches that,
in the case of South Vietnamese villages suspected of
being susceptible to Communist influence, we drive
their inhabitants out, burn their houses and destroy
their crops, and imprison them in concentration
camps for which we have cleverly invented the
euphemism "strategic villages." "Some families," says
Bigart (March 29, 1962), "had been allowed to
carry away beds, tables and benches before their
houses were burned. Others had almost nothing but
the clothes on their backs. A young woman stood
expressionless as she recounted how the troops had
burned the families' two tons of rice." Well, Sher-
man did this in the South, and many people think
he was justified, but why should we be doing it to
the Vietnamese, who live not next to us but next
door to China, for the purpose of convincing these
uninstructed peasants that the American Way of
Life is freer and more desirable than that imposed
by the Communist ideology?

But before going on with the history of chemical and biological warfare—biological warfare is the infection of the enemy with deadly contagious diseases—it may be well to explain what at the present time we are prepared to do to an enemy (whom we always, of course, assume to be ready to do the same things to us). The Germans, in the course of the second war, discovered a new order of gases, "nerve gases," which, according to the British Service Manual, are "colorless liquids" that "in vapor form are invisible" and in some cases, "virtually odorless." They penetrated clothing, and no respirator could be effective against them; "a few drops of liquid on the bare skin may kill within half an hour." A German report on these gases describes the effects of one of them, in an experiment on a herd of goats: "The goats were violently ill, then became rampant maniacs and killed each other in a fury of uncontrollable destruction." Before 1945, says Philip Noel-Baker in his book *The Arms Race*, the Western Allies had these gases, too, "and all the leading governments possess them now." The Germans at the end of the war had three factories making these gases and Hitler had given orders to use them; but the Nazi Minister of Production testified at the Nüremburg trials that he had disobeyed these orders: "In military circles there was certainly no one in favor of gas warfare. All sensible people turned gas

warfare down as being utterly insane, since, in view
of your superiority in the air, it would not be long
before it would bring the most terrible catastrophe
upon German cities." The recent development of
missiles has made the delivery of these gases easier,
and the Chief Chemical Officer of the United States
Army went on record in 1955 as believing that
chemical weapons had already become as formi-
dable as A-bombs, and that by loosing these invisible
vapors, "mental derangement might be deliberately
inspired."

The substances used in flame-throwers and napalm
bombs are also a department of chemical warfare.
The Germans and afterwards the French used flame-
throwers in the first war: these squirted a burning
liquid. But in the second war, incendiary bombs
were much more serious weapons. It was by dropping these bombs that the Nazis obliterated Guernica
and Coventry, and by our own use of these weapons
we did far more damage in Tokyo than we did in
Hiroshima and Nagasaki—we burned up fifteen
square miles of the city and 83,000 persons, mostly
civilians. According to the United States Strategic
Bombing Survey, we attacked with incendiary
bombs sixty-five Japanese cities in all and totally
destroyed half of them. When the Allies in combination attacked forty-nine German towns, most of the
devastation was accomplished by holocaust rather

than by blasting. The British in a nine-day raid on Hamburg destroyed 75% of the city and burned to death or poisoned with carbon monoxide between 70,000 and 100,000 people. In the meantime, we had discovered napalm, which the Germans had not yet thought of. Napalm is a kind of jelly saturated with gasoline, which is ignited by the bursting of the bomb. Its great advantage is that it sticks to whatever it touches. It was used by our army in Korea and is said to have been used in Vietnam, though I have seen no reliable report of this. Its effect on human beings has been described by a BBC correspondent in Korea: "In front of us a curious figure was standing a little crouched, legs straddled, arms held out from his sides. He had no eyes, and the whole of his body, nearly all of which was visible through tatters of burned rags, was covered with a hard black crust speckled with yellow pus. A Korean woman by his side began to speak, and the interpreter said: 'He has to stand, sir, cannot sit or lie.' He had to stand because he was no longer covered with a skin, but with a crust like crackling which broke easily." The correspondent, Mr. R. Cutforth, author of a book called *Korean Reporter*, adds that he would rather be killed by napalm than by phosphorus and flame-throwers, "which have been with us for years. . . . Napalm reaches a temperature of more than 1,000 C. in a few seconds and the vast ma-

jority of its victims are killed outright." By this reasoning, says Mr. Noel-Baker, by way of whose books
I have been quoting Mr. Cutforth, "the atomic bomb
at Hiroshima was, in its immediate effect, less terrible than the fire-raids on Hamburg and Tokyo."
One needs to carry this only a little farther to con-
clude, as I believe some have done, that to wipe out
the Communist cities with H-bombs would amount
to what are called "mercy killings," and it follows
that it would be worthwhile to sacrifice our own
cities, as we should surely have to do, in the cause
of putting out of their misery these misguided Communist millions.

In the department of contagious diseases—that is,
biological warfare—we are working on ingenious
methods to propagate epidemics in the following
categories. I quote the list from Norman Cousin's
In Place of Folly, but it is to be found in a balder
version in a study of *Chemical-Biological-Radiologi-
cal (CBR) Warfare and Its Disarmament Aspects*
prepared by the Subcommittee on Disarmament of the
Committee of Foreign Relations, and published by
the United States government on August 29, 1960.

"1. *Viruses.* Epidemics that can be transmitted in
war through the use of viruses include psittacosis,
Russian spring-summer encephalitis, Venezuelan
equine encephalitis, influenza, pleuropneumonia.

"2. *Protozoa*. Amoebic dysentery and malaria are among the diseases in this category. However, protozoa are not so easy to grow or transmit as microorganisms in other categories.

"3. *Rickettsiae*. Transmittable diseases in this group include Q fever, Rocky Mountain spotted fever, dengue fever, Rift Valley fever, typhus, p typhoid. Manufacture and transmission of these diseases in war are considered attainable and realistic.

"4. *Bacteria*. Among the potent types useful in war are those that produce plague, cholera, smallpox, diphtheria, tularemia, anthrax, brucellosis.

"5. *Fungi*. The principal use of fungi in war would be against fruits and vegetables. However, human beings are vulnerable to coccidioidomycosis or Joaquin Valley fever, transmittable through fungus."

A somewhat fuller list is to be found on pp. 14–15 of the government pamphlet quoted above. This includes, also, the propagation of many insect and other pests—including the army-worm, the cotton boll weevil and the giant African snail—which hitherto we had been trying to exterminate.

At a meeting of the American Chemical Society on April 6, 1960, it was explained by Dr. LeRoy D. Fothergill, special advisor to the U.S. Army Biological Laboratory, that, "The overt means of dissemination is aerosol spray in a biological cloud that is invisible, odorless and tasteless. It permeates most structures, searches out and infects all targets permeable or breathing. It establishes new foci of contagious disease in animals, insects, birds, and people, and contaminates hospitals, kitchens, restaurants, and warehouses. The infection of an entire continent by biological clouds is possible under proper meteorological conditions. Covert means of dissemination through saboteurs are almost endlessly imaginable and nearly as practical."

Among these covert means, one gathers from an Army publication, the circulation of which has been limited—*U.S. Army Capability in the Space Age*—is the use of certain insects as disease-carriers. These insects are being bred in great quantities at Fort Detrick in Frederick, Maryland, where bateriological researches are going on. We have here been enriching our armory with an abundance of well-fed mosquitos infected with yellow fever and malaria; fleas infected with plague; ticks with tularcmia, relapsing fever and Colorado fever; and houseflies with cholera, anthrax and dysentery. Nor are the diseases of plants neglected: we have developed effective methods to kill the crops of wheat, barley, oats, rye, rice and cotton. It has been found feasible, it seems, to spread wheat-rust on the wings of larks. "I should like to say at this point," said Dr. Fothergill in one of his addresses, "that many of these aerobiological instruments and techniques have been developed to a remarkable state of technical perfection." An experiment has been made by the Chemical Corps of dropping two hundred thousand mosquitoes in special containers all around a certain airbase in Florida which is usually free from mosquitoes. It was found that "within a few days, a high percentage of the people living on and around the base had been bitten many times. Had the mosquitoes been carrying a disease such as yellow fever, the Chemical Corps believes that most of the local inhabitants would have been infected."* This artificial cultivation of yellow fever and cholera epidemics, after the centuries when humanity has suffered from them and when cures and controls have at last been found, must be the most macabre irony of medical history—especially when one considers that efforts are now being made to intensify the virulence of these diseases and to render them proof against antibiotics. The one thing that is difficult to deal with is a technique to prevent them from crossing frontiers and so depopulating the countries that are spreading them.

* These data about insect carriers are derived from an article by Walter Schneir in the *Reporter* of October 1, 1959.

The Soft Sell for CBR

The story of the official handling of CBR in relation to the general public is interesting as one of the most disturbing examples of the dishonesty of which our government has recently been capable in concealing or disguising from this public what our war department is actually up to.

A Major General Brock Chisholm, who was the first Director-General of the World Health Organization, told a press conference at the UN headquarters in 1949 that "most of the world's inhabitants will be wiped out in any future war in which virulent bacteria now developed are used as a weapon. . . . Bacteriological weapons, developed late in the Second World War, could wipe out all human life in a given area within six hours and yet leave the area habitable afterwards."* In another statement, made in September, 1957, he said that, "There is at present probably no exchange of information between any nations on this subject, although the major military nations all know that the others are carrying on research. The military authorities of all countries have

* *Montreal Gazette,* Oct. 14, 1949.

almost always pursued a policy of total secrecy. In 1939, an American published a somewhat superficial book describing the general character of the biological and chemical weapons which then existed. The United States General Staff authorities traced down every copy and confiscated it; not one remained available to the public."

In the course of the second war (June 8, 1943), President Roosevelt made the following statement on the "use of poisonous or noxious gases or other inhumane devices of warfare": "Use of such weapons has been outlawed by the general opinion of civilized mankind. This country has not used them, and I hope that we never will be compelled to use them. I state categorically that we shall under no circumstances resort to the use of such weapons unless they are first used by our enemies." But the military objected to this. Why should we commit ourselves thus to refraining from any advantage which might enable us to forestall the enemy? The whole issue was left in obscurity till the latter part of 1959. From then on through 1960, it was given a certain amount of publicity. The Pentagon's program of expenditure for 1960 on chemical and bacteriological warfare was $7,000,000; it would need for the following year $7,600,000; and it predicted that in seven or eight years it would be needing $200,000,000 a year. The public would have to be recon-

ciled to the idea that such expenditures were necessary, that such methods were humane and innocuous
—since it was only proposed to use gases that would
render the victims irresponsible or reduce them to
temporary unconsciousness. A Major General William M. Creasy, the former head of the Chemical
Corps, is quoted in *This Week* in the New York
Herald Tribune of May 17, 1959, as having made a
joyous announcement: "There is no question in my
mind that for the first time in history there is the
promise—even the probability—that war will not
necessarily mean death." The publicity campaign
was, on this account, given the delightful name of
"Operation Blue Skies": hope for mankind at last!
High military officers made speeches and testified at
Congressional hearings, where the effects of the drugs
on animals were demonstrated; articles by retired officers, who could not be held accountable, were
contributed to magazines, and journalists and editors
were told that certain officers might now be inter-
viewed, and that hitherto classified information
would now be made accessible to the public. It did
not seem to occur to those who were handling the
Chemical Corps's publicity that these announcements
might not always make a good impression, and that
the whole truth was bound to come out. They did
not foresee such articles as that by Walter Schneir in
the *Reporter*, with its subheading "Love That

Germ!" Though every attempt was made not to let anything ugly appear, this soon proved to be impossible, since everything about CBR was ugly. For one thing, the Pentagon itself was unable to repress its enthusiasm at the prospect of exterminating by epidemic—a device which had the same advantage as the projected neutron bomb: it would leave machines and buildings available for practical use after the operators and inhabitants had been putrefied.

As for the scientists who had been working in this department, their attitude toward their work seems ambiguous and rather troubled, as we find it in the papers they read, in the April of 1960, at one of the international conferences at Pugwash, Nova Scotia, which included Soviet scientists as well as Western ones, and at a symposium held at a meeting of the American Chemical Society in April, 1960, (both summarized in the June, 1960, issue of the *Bulletin of the Atomic Scientists*, which is specially devoted to this subject, and the latter also dealt with in an article in the *Nation* of April 30, 1960). One gets the impression that these experts are sometimes trying to warn the public of the horrors in store for humanity if their researches are allowed to proceed, of the deliberate setbacks to civilization for the preparation of which they have been employed; and that sometimes, as impassioned technicians, they are boasting of the marvels that can now be accomplished; and there is also, of course, an emphasis on the dangers of the depredations which the Russians, by similar devices, would be able to accomplish against us. At a preliminary press conference to the meeting of the American Chemical Society, Dr. Paul Weiss of the Rockefeller Institute, a member of the President's Scientific Advisory Committee, exclaimed to the reporters: "Don't ask me any questions. I know too much I shouldn't tell!"; and then went on to say: "We must convince the scientific community that chemical and biological warfare is not a dirty business. It is no worse than other means of killing. There is no excuse for scientists' regarding it as degrading, particularly in the light of its public-health aspects." The quotation in the *Nation* breaks off at this point. One would like to hear something more about these "public-health aspects" that put such activities in a better light. It is more wholesome, one can only suppose, to spread a spot of cholera or anthrax than to handicap future generations by the degenerative effects of radioactivity. When Dr. Fothergill, mentioned above, was questioned about the "vigil of protest," in which about a thousand people participated, that had been carried on at Fort Detrick for a year by the Fellowship of Reconciliation, he replied, "We pay no attention to them, and neither does the town." And the whole purpose of these proceedings of the Amerìcan Chemical Society seems to have been to put forward the importance of impressing upon the public the necessity for "an effective level of preparedness." The scientists at Pugwash, on the other hand, seem rather to be trying to suggest the undesirability, on account of its destructiveness and possible uselessness, of chemical and bacteriological warfare. The Soviet scientists here are more outspoken than those of the West. Says A. A. Imshevetsky, the director of microbiology for the Soviet Academy of Sciences: "Scientists and especially microbiologists working in countries throughout the world should combat the preparations for biological warfare, which will bring mankind suffering, disease and annihilation." Says M. M. Dubinin, also of the Soviet Academy of Sciences, "Soviet scientists, just as all Soviet people, look upon chemical and biological warfare measures as weapons of mass destruction, the use of which is incompatible with the demands of humaneness and the norms of international law. They decisively condemn exhortations and efforts to spread preparations for chemical and bacteriological warfare." But how free are Soviet scientists "to combat" these preparations? How free, for that matter, are our own? It is difficult to understand why it should not be quite possible, in the assertedly "free world" of the United States, for chemists and microbiologists who find their government work distasteful or "degrading" to resign and find other employment.

The official point of view is expressed in the report of a House Committee on Science and Astronautics called *Research in CBR*. This report complains that "at the present time, CBR research is supported at a level equivalent to only one-thousandth of our total defense budget," and recommends that "in the light of its potentialities . . . serious consideration be given to the request of defense officials that this support be at least trebled. Only an increase of such size is likely to speed research to a level of attainment compatible with the efforts of the Communist nations."

Since 1960, however, CBR has had little publicity. It need never have taken the trouble to try to make its activities attractive by Madison Avenue methods. The apathy and timidity of the American public gave it carte blanche to go ahead. Nobody wanted to worry about such grisly matters, so nobody wanted to hear about them. I discovered in 1961, when I was looking the subject up, that even people who read the papers and who were otherwise in a position to know about current happenings expressed incredulity when I told them about what was going on. An awkward result of this practice of not talking about the subject is that it has been left quite unclear how to handle it in connection with possible disarmament. CBR weapons have been mentioned, but barely, in the various disarmament proposals, yet the problems of inspection they present have never been discussed in detail. According to the conclusions of the Pugwash Conference, such inspections would be "incomparably more difficult" than those for the control of atomic weapons, of which the places of manufacture and the experimental tests are bound to be more or less conspicuous. In the case of these other weapons, one can choose among so many possibilities of diseases and noxious gases, that it would be hard to pin down what was being done. One would never know where to look. "The raw materials are cheap and can be processed in ordinary chemical or microbiological laboratories under conditions where it would be most difficult to detect violations."

How Free Is the Free World?

I have said that it was difficult to understand, in what we call our free world, how it can come about that a scientist who has been working on CBR but is dubious about the morality of what he is doing should not find it in his power to resign. But how free are we citizens of this free world to resign from the gigantic and demented undertakings to which our government has got us committed? The truth is that the people of the United States are at the present time dominated and driven by two kinds of officially propagated fear: fear of the Soviet Union and fear of the income tax. These two terrors have been adjusted so as to complement one another and thus to keep the citizen of our free society under the strain of a double pressure from which he finds himself unable to escape—like the man in the old Western story, who, chased into a narrow ravine by a buffalo, is confronted with a grizzly bear. If we fail to accept the tax, the Russian buffalo will butt and trample us, and if we try to defy the tax, the federal bear will crush us. People often become panic-stricken, it seems, in the presence of IRS agents, and have sometimes been known to faint. They feel that they are up against an official police which possesses unlimited power and from which there is no appeal. This is not quite correct, since one can sue the government; but not everyone can afford to do this, and if one cannot, one has to submit to the exactions of an all-powerful bureaucracy.

The effect on American life of this double intimidation has been frustrating to the individual to the point of stultification or fury. And the fact that the bulk of the nation's funds is being spent, as the new budget shows, on the exploration of space, the arrears from previous wars and the preparation, in prospect of future wars, of the instruments of wholesale destruction and deliberate contamination —the fact that what we do and what we make goes mostly not for life and enlightenment on this planet on which we have not yet found out how to get along decently with one another but for the propagation of darkness and death, for ourselves as well as for the enemy, has been poisoning American society to an extent of which most of us are not fully aware. We amuse ourselves with labor-saving devices that compute or wash dishes for us; we drug ourselves with the slop of TV programs or driving on monotonous highways in cars of abominable design; we may hope for a moment of enjoyment from bottled and pre-mixed cocktails or an outdoor grill in the suburbs or a movie that shows lovers in bed or someone getting lashed or bashed. (With all this, in the meantime, such simple commodities as nylon stockings and safety razor blades have, in order to keep their market up, been made to deteriorate so in quality that the stockings, which used to last for months, now run at the slightest contact and the blades—which, as manu-factured in England, will give you a dozen smooth shaves—can now hardly be made to serve once without an effortful scraping.) But the United States, for

all its so much advertized comforts, is today an uncomfortable place. It is idle for our "leaders" and
"liberals" to talk about the necessity for Americans to
recover their old idealism, to consecrate themselves
again to their mission of liberation. Our national mission, if our budget proves anything, has taken on co-
lossal dimensions, but in its interference in foreign
countries and its support of oppressive regimes, it has
hardly been a liberating mission, and the kind of
idealism involved is becoming insane and intolerant in
the manner of the John Birch Society. Even those
who do not give much conscious thought to what has
been taking place are discouraged and blocked in
their work or alienated from their normal ambitions
by the paralyzing chill of a national effort directed
toward a blind dead end which is all the more horri-
fying and haunting for being totally inconsecutive
with their daily lives and inapprehensible to their
imaginations. The accomplished, the intelligent, the
well-informed go on in their useful professions that
require high integrity and intellect, but they suffer
more and more from the crowding of an often un-
avowed constraint which may prevent them from
allowing themselves to become too intelligent and
well-informed or may drive them to indulge their
skills in gratuitous and futile exercises. One notices
in the conversation of this professional class certain
inhibitions on free expression, a tacit understanding

that certain matters had better not be brought into discussion, which sometimes makes one feel in such talk a kind of fundamental frivolity. The ordinary American who is more or less well-off, or who hopes to be more or less well-off, by the standards of his social group may not know that the mosquitoes he is keeping away by the smoke from his outdoor grill or the fleas he is powdering his dog to get rid of are being carefully reared at Fort Detrick to be loaded with yellow fever and plague germs, and that this work is being paid for in part through an allotment of the money he is earning which might otherwise be devoted to getting his children better educated and dressed; but he does undoubtedly know that a considerable slice of this money goes to pay for nuclear tests and an accumulation of weapons for prospective bombings—and he may even have reflected that if these bombings do not in the long run take place, it must have been entirely wasted. He may also have some sense of the danger that any possible survivors from a bombed area may for generations give birth to defective offspring—which will somewhat resemble, I gather, an unfortunate swarm of flies I once saw which had hatched in an outhouse near a box of lime and which, with legs and wings partly eaten, could only miserably and limpingly crawl, never emerging from the lime-strewn outhouse. Tougher members of the population—among upper and lower brackets—have privately taken the stand that they are damned if they are going to lie down and take it when they are persecuted and spied upon and rooked by that son of a bitch Uncle Sam, who pretends that he is saving them from those Russians that live half the world's breadth away. They are contemptuous of the danger that they run of being liable to reprisals or prosecutions, and they figure out subterfuges for beating the game. I have said that the technicians were comparatively happy; but in the case of a man with an acute realization, by way of imagination or of personal experience, of the objects for which he has been working, he may, like Leo Szilard make an effort to repress the forces he has helped to release or, like certain of the CBR scientists, obliquely try to tip off the public as to the nature of the projects it has been subsidizing.

The Case of Major Eatherly

One of the most significant cases of the revolted technician is that of Major Claude R. Eatherly, who was Commander of the bomber group that blasted

Hiroshima and Nagasaki. He seems to have been unique among bombers in afterwards having paused to take account of his responsibility and in attempting to do something to expiate it. What happened to him may be read in a book called *Burning Conscience*, which contains his correspondence with Dr. Günther Anders, an Austrian philosopher and pacifist, who had read about his case and become interested in him. The first of the bombs dropped, says Eatherly, writing of this mission, had been intended to destroy a bridge near the Japanese military headquarters, "thus convincing," says Eatherly, "the Japanese military that they should sign a peace treaty and end the terrible war,"* but it missed the target by some 3,000 feet and destroyed the town of Hiroshima. Eatherly knew that the mistake had been made, and "after I saw the destruction, I didn't want to go over Nagasaki, but I went." He had already before this raid done thirteen months of continuous

* At a decisive meeting of an "Interim Committee" in the Pentagon on May 31, 1945, the minutes report that:
"After much discussion concerning various types of targets and the effects to be produced, the Secretary [Stimson] expressed the conclusion, on which there was general agreement, that we could not give the Japanese any warning; that we could not concentrate on a civilian area; but that we could make a profound psychological impression on as many of the inhabitants as possible. At the suggestion of Dr. Conant, the Secretary agreed that the most desirable target would be a vital war plant employing a large number of workers and closely surrounded by workers' houses."
(Quoted by Knebel and Bailey in *Look*.)

patrol duty over the South Pacific, and when he returned from this last mission, he broke down and for days would not speak to anyone. He then made the resolution, as he afterwards wrote, to devote the rest of his life to "destroying the causes of war" and to "the banishment of all nuclear weapons." But how could he live up to this? "Even if one harmed one fellow man" . . . Dr. Anders was later to write him, "it is, although the deed can be seen at a glance, no easy task to 'digest' it. But here it is something else. You happen to have left 200,000 dead behind you. And how should one be able to mobilize a pain which embraces 200,000? How should one repent 200,000? Not only you cannot do it, no one can do it. However desperately we may repent it, pain and repentance remain inadequate." The situation in which Eatherly found himself was so new that a human being had no way of adjusting himself to it. At first, he travelled around the country speaking to pacifist groups, and, he says, "appeared on television with Christian leaders." But, he adds, "I am not wanted in our schools and universities." He took a job with an oil company in Texas, but then began sending money to Hiroshima and writing letters to the Japanese, now condemning, now apologizing for himself. On the announcement, in 1950, that the hydrogen bomb was under way, he made an attempt to commit suicide in a hotel room by an overdose of sleeping pills. He tried manual labor in the oil fields in the hope of thus by physical activity being able to keep his mind off his guilt; then he resorted to a strange course of conduct. He had not allowed himself to be fêted when he returned to his home town in Texas, and he now set out to try to discredit the popular myth of the war hero. He began committing petty crimes from which he derived no benefit: he forged a check for a small amount and contributed the money to a fund for the children of Hiroshima. He held up banks and broke into post offices without ever taking anything. "To most people," he afterwards wrote, "my method of rebellion against war is that of an insane person"; but in "no other way could I have made people realize that nuclear war is moral degeneration as well as physical destruction." At one point, he brought himself to work for six weeks as salesman for a sewing-machine company, and then again tried to kill himself by slashing his wrists.

He was of course by now extremely neurotic, but how much of this was due to the ordeals of the war and to the agonies of conscience it had left with him? His wife made him go to a psychiatrist, and since then he has spent most of his time in the Veterans' Administration Hospital in Waco, Texas. At first, he went there voluntarily, but later his brother committed him, and he was kept in the asylum against his will. He wrote and published articles against nuclear warfare, and it is obvious that the Air Force has made every effort to keep him under control and to create the impression that he is quite insane. But there is nothing in these published letters to suggest that he was really deranged. Nor is there anything hysterical in them. He corresponds with pacifist organizations and follows with solicitous interest the case of the physicist Dr. Linus Pauling, who was also a protester against nuclear warfare and who incurred—till he won the Nobel Prize—a determined persecution by a Senate internal security committee by refusing to supply it with the names of other persons who shared his opinions. Eatherly talks of writing a book and giving the proceeds "most to Japan, some to Germany . . . and to other countries, set up in a foundation where income tax can't touch it and build a bomb with it." He gives of his past actions what seems a responsible account and he seems to have a realistic grasp of his present situation. But his letters are censored and suppressed. He explains in one written to Anders in November, 1960, that he has tried to get himself released by resorting to legal channels. "That failed because the Air Force filed a commitment against me indefinitely, and then had the hospital notify the court not to serve a summons on me so I could not take it to court. Last Wednesday I talked with my doctor, and he told me I was in the unfortunate position of being so well-known and famous that I must stop my writings against nuclear weapons and using my influence in foreign countries through U.S. magazines. He said that he could do nothing to help me, that he and the hospital staff had to take orders from the Air Force and the State Department. I asked him if they intended to keep me here, and he said yes. . . . This country is much like many other countries. It is nearly impossible to go against the military." He now escaped but was recognized at an airport, then traced by the police and brought back. He was now put in the violent ward, where, as he said, many of the patients did not know their own names. "The only people with whom I can talk are the wardens." A man from the Waco *News Tribune,* who attended the court hearing preliminary to this, a hearing before a board of psychiatrists which the army itself had appointed, reported (for a French newspaper) that "Eatherly's attitude was admirable. . . . He answered the questions put to him directly and without difficulty . . . mostly with a brief, soldierly 'Yes, sir . . . No, sir.' " The same reporter wrote elsewhere that "Eatherly was probably the most intelligent person in the whole court room."

One of the most striking things in these letters is Eatherly's declaration that, "Whilst in no sense, I hope, either a religious or a political fanatic, I have for some time felt convinced that the crisis in which we are all involved is one calling for a thorough re-ëxamination of our whole scheme of values and of loyalties. In the past it has sometimes been possible for men to 'coast along' without posing to themselves too many searching questions about the way they are accustomed to think and to act—but it is reasonably clear that our age is not one of these. On the contrary, I believe that we are rapidly approaching a situation in which we shall be compelled to reëxamine our willingness to surrender responsibility for our thoughts and actions to some social institution such as the political party, trade union, church or State. None of these institutions are adequately equipped to offer infallible advice on moral issues and their claim to offer such advice needs therefore to be challenged."

More "normal" was undoubtedly the remark of one of Eatherly's Hiroshima companions, and who was not troubled by any compunction: "For me it was just a bigger bomb." This man might have pleaded, if pressed further, like Eichmann, that he was merely a cog in the great machine, that he was simply obeying orders. And so may plead every official who takes orders in the Pentagon or the CIA or the IRS, when the deforming and cremating blasts are set off to make a sterile waste of a country in which other human beings live, when the missiles are at last released that exterminate these human beings by communicating contagious diseases or that cook them alive with showers of fire. And every one of the non-official public may plead, as did the German civilians, that we were leaving it all to the government and had not grasped what was going to happen; the indifference and the cravenness of this non-official public will then look as ignominious as that of the German civilians who did not or would not know about the gas ovens and tortures of the Nazis.

The Strategy of Tax Refusal

Now, how is one to struggle against this situation? Go on strike and refuse to pay taxes? The persons who have given this problem most thought are the members of the peace organizations, and discussions of it may be found in the *Peacemaker*, published by the Peacemakers group, and *Liberation*, initiated by the Fellowship of Reconciliation. The alternative procedures are these: (1) Arrange to be self-employed, so that nothing can be withheld from your earnings, and see to it that your income is never allowed to rise above the taxable level. Dr. A. J.

Muste, the secretary emeritus of the Fellowship of Reconciliation, has, in his own case, refused to accept this solution. "Voluntarily keeping one's income down," he writes, "does not commend itself to me as a form of tax protest. I do not see how one can in effect recognize that a government may determine one's standard of living or think that permitting the government to do so constitutes a significant protest against war taxation." (2) Pay only that percentage of one's tax that represents the portion of the national revenue not devoted to preparations for war. The objection to this is that the same proportion of what you do pay will still go for these preparations. (3) Do not file, but write to the tax bureau and explain to them what you are doing and why you believe you are justified in doing it. Be respectful to the authorities and comply with summonses. (4) Do nothing about filing, refuse to obey summonses, and take the consequences. What happens when one or the other of these last two courses of conduct is adopted may be illustrated by the histories of individual cases.

Dr. Muste, a Presbyterian minister turned labor organizer and once head of Brookwood Labor College, whom I first knew and learned to respect in my days as a labor reporter when he was working with the independent coal miners' unions, now devotes himself to the campaign for peace and is one of the editors of *Liberation*, a monthly magazine mainly occupied with the interests of this movement, and National Chairman of the Committee for Non-Violent Action. Since Dr. Muste is an ordained minister, the small salary he received for this work was not subject to the withholding tax; but a young woman who was acting as his secretary had inhibitions, not shared by her colleagues, about contributing to nuclear warfare by allowing a part of her salary to be withheld. She resigned, and Dr. Muste decided that he ought to take a stand himself. He ceased filing, but "notified the authorities each year of what I was doing and why." Muste's age, his unimpeachable character and his obvious moral sincerity as well as, no doubt, the knowledge that he could owe very little or nothing have evidently induced the tax people to treat him with unusual leniency. They first came to examine the books of the Fellowship of Reconciliation, then they let the matter rest for two years. Dr. Muste was eventually, however, asked to come for an interview, which lasted for two hours and was tape-recorded. He was requested to sign a transcript, and he consented to do so if he could read it first. This was the last he ever heard about the transcript. Years passed, then attempts were made to get him to sign a return. This would have been a token acknowledgment on his part which would have allowed them to drop the case; but Dr. Muste refused to sign, and the affair was still allowed to drag on, till at last the offender was haled into the tax court. At the end of a year, the tax court made a ruling that a fraud had not been committed. The next year no payment was made, and it was threatened to levy on his social security and on his pension from the Fellowship of Reconciliation; but so far nothing further has happened.

Some of the other recalcitrants got harsher treatment. Miss Eroscanna Robinson, a Negro, the recreational director of a Chicago community center, is an athlete of such calibre that she was chosen to represent the United States in a track meet in which we competed with Russia. She refused on the ground that she was unwilling "to be used as a political pawn," as she would be if, appearing abroad side by side with white American contestants, she were made to convey the impression that Negroes in the United States were given an equal status with white people. She has, also, on the same grounds as Muste, refused to report her income to the government—as the result of which, in February, 1960, she was sentenced, for "criminal contempt," to a year and a day in jail. In prison, she went on a hunger strike and was forcibly fed through the nose. As a result of her unwillingness, as was charged, to conform with prison regulations, she was held incommunicado, forbidden to receive visitors or to write or receive letters. Another war protester, Walter Gormly, a consulting engineer

of Mt. Vernon, Iowa, served a federal sentence in the
last war for refusing to coöperate with the draft,
and began at that time to refuse to pay the federal
income tax. He has since been in continual hot water. The authorities first took his station-wagon and
sold it at public auction; then more recently, confiscated a bank balance of $180—though the district
assistant director of the tax bureau has been quoted
by the Desmoines *Register* as admitting, "We really
don't know what his income is. There is much doubt
that he has sufficient income to require him to file a
tax return or to pay income taxes." But, "since
Gormly refuses to supply agents with income information, the burden of disproving the tax claims is
upon Gormly." The offender retorted by explaining:
"I talked with Ernest Bacon, area director, and other
officials . . . I asked them to show me the legal basis
for the assessment against me and did not get a satisfactory explanation." He then began passing out
leaflets of protest at the entrance of the Desmoines
IRS offices, exhibiting himself as an example of what
the government could do to a tax delinquent: "Since
the Internal Revenue Service employees do not care
whether or not I starve, I am going on a hunger
strike to show them what a starving man looks like."
(I can sympathize with Mr. Gormly. When my
sources of income were all cut off, my lawyer suggested that I might make an impression by going on

poor relief.) He was arrested in June, 1962, on a charge of "loitering in a federal building." The judge sent him off to prison for a psychiatric examination, and threatened that if he did not behave himself, "he would commit him to a mental institution." (We have taken so many leaves from the Soviets' book—in the way of persecution for unorthodox opinion, guilt by association, etc.—that it is possible to wonder whether the Soviets may have not taken a leaf from ours in the practice they have lately adopted of disposing of their heretical authors, as well as of the Captain Ivanov who was involved in the Profumo scandal, by consigning them to insane asylums.) In prison, Mr. Gormly continued to fast and was given intravenous nourishment. At last he was quietly released, with no bail demanded and no date set for trial.

The most conspicuous and impressive of these cases—though none of them, certainly, has had much publicity—is that of the Reverend Maurice F. McCrackin, the pastor of West Cincinnati-St. Barnabas church of Cincinnati. Dr. McCrackin, who comes of a family of Presbyterian ministers, has always had a very strong religious vocation. After graduating from the seminary in 1930, he first became a missionary and served for five years in Iran, where he was asked awkward questions by the school boys: if Jesus was the Prince of Peace, why was it that the Christian Crusaders had made the streets of Jerusalem

run with Mohammedan blood?* Returning to the
United States, he spent five years in the oil and steel
town of Hammond, Indiana, during which he made
trips to Chicago to attend the meetings there of the
Fellowship of Reconciliation and of a Pacifist Ministers' Fellowship. He was "thrilled," he says, when
in October, 1940, he heard the news of the refusal of
eight students at Union Theological Seminary in
New York to register for military service, and
though he filled out a blank himself, he accompanied
his registration with a protest. But he was afterwards
troubled by conscience at the thought that he was
encouraging others to be conscientious objectors
when he, as an ordained minister, was exempted from
the draft himself. He then went into settlement
work, first in Chicago, then in Cincinnati, as co-
pastor of the amalgamated church named above.
"Soon we organized a Community Council and tried
to come to grips with community problems. Ties in
church and settlement house were growing strong
and meaningful. Camp Joy was opened to children
of all races and creeds, and with integrated camping
and a racially mixed staff, children and teen-age
young people grew in self-assurance and in respect and love for one another." I have heard
Dr. McCrackin speak, and he struck me as a

* I am following an autobiographical document—*Pilgrimage
of a Conscience*—written by Dr. McCrackin.

logical, vigorous and very determined man. When
our bombs were dropped on the Japanese, and it
became apparent that our government was manu-
facturing more and worse bombs to operate on
an even more destructive scale, Dr. McCrackin
was dismayed at the thought that if at Hiroshima
a whole human community had been burnt out
like a colony of tentworms—"nurses, teachers, domestic workers, laborers, and secretaries . . . babies,
children, young people and adults, living together,
playing and working together and praying together"
—then the institutions in Cincinnati to which he was
devoting himself—"churches, settlement houses,
schools"—could easily be obliterated in the same
way. He had to take account of the fact that he had
been giving to the United States government a part
of the money that made this possible, and at this
point he began the practice of withholding from the
payment of his income tax the amount that went for
war preparations and contributing this amount "to
such causes as the American Friends Service Committee's program and to other works of mercy and
reconciliation." "As time went on, I realized, however, that this was not accomplishing its purpose, because year after year the government ordered my
bank to release money from my account to pay the
tax I had held back. I then closed my checking
account and by some method better known to the

Internal Revenue Service than to me, it was discovered that I had money in a savings and loan company. Orders were given to this firm, under threat of prosecution, to surrender from my account the amount the government said I owed. I then realized suddenly how far the government is now invading individual rights and privileges: money is given in trust to a firm to be kept in safety and the government coerces this firm's trustees into violation of that trust. But even more evil than this invasion of rights is the violence done to the individual's conscience in forcing him to give financial support to a thing he feels so deeply is wrong."

He then decided that he was not going to supply the government with any more information which could be used by it to frustrate his purpose. In August of 1958, he was served a summons to appear and answer questions about his taxes for the years 1955–57. He replied to the tax bureau as follows: "I have received your summons to appear before you on September 10th. I must decline to do so. The Department of Internal Revenue exercises a power of coercion which threatens the liberty of the individual, violates conscience and jeopardizes the life of our free institutions. I believe that it is to the best interests of our country that drastic changes be made both in the use made of tax money and in the practices of the Internal Revenue Service Department. My conscience tells me that I can neither pay my taxes nor coöperate with you in your effort to collect them. I therefore cannot meet with you on September 10.

"Mankind is now threatened with extinction. Two powerful military nations, Russia and the United States, though affirming they believe in and want peace, are daily leading us closer to the brink of war. Some way this death march must be stopped.

"During these past years and particularly in the last two, I have learned how far the arm of government extends into the life of the citizen and the church. Bank accounts can be appropriated, safety deposit boxes sealed up, cars, houses and other personal property seized to meet the demands of the Department of Internal Revenue, no matter how conscientiously opposed the individual may be to answering these demands."

U.S. marshals now came to arrest him, with a warrant that read: "You are ordered to bring the body of Maurice F. McCrackin"—he told them that they could take his body, but he would not voluntarily go with them: "You cannot take my conscience nor my spirit into custody." They carried him to the county jail, and in due course he was indicted for contempt of court (he had refused to stand before the judge). He was sentenced to six months in Leavenworth, and, declining to make an appeal, Dr. McCrackin served out this sentence.

A campaign was being waged against him, even before his arrest, by the Southern segregationists and the American Legion: the inevitable accusations of "Red" affiliations were made; and when Dr. McCrackin was released, he found himself suspended from the communion of his church by the presbytery of Cincinnati. The charges against him are interesting:

"(1). The Rev. Maurice F. McCrackin has resisted the ordinances of God, in that upon pretense of Christian liberty he has opposed the civil lawful power, and the lawful exercise of it, contrary to the constitution of the United Presbyterian Church in the United States of America. (Confession of Faith Chapter XX, paragraph 4.) [Withholding part of his income, refusing to file and refusing to obey the summons.]

"(2) The Rev. Maurice F. McCrackin has published erroneous opinions and maintained practices which are destructive to the external peace and order which Christ hath established in the Church, contrary to the Constitution of the United Presbyterian Church in the United States of America. (Confession of Faith, Chapter XX, paragraph 4.) [Making use of his pulpit to urge others to follow his example.]

"(3) The Rev. Maurice F. McCrackin has failed to obey the lawful commands and to be subject to the authority of the civil magistrates, contrary to the Constitution of the United Presbyterian Church in the United States of America. (Confession of Faith, Chapter XXIII, paragraph 4.) [The same offenses as above, plus a notification to the IRS that he proposed to continue his disobedience.]"

On February 19 of this year, he received the following notice of deposal: "Whereas Maurice F. McCrackin has been convicted by sufficient proof of the sin of obstinate impenitence and, by his sin and unfaithfulness, has brought reproach on the cause of his Master ['Render therefore unto Caesar the things which are Caesar's'?], we, therefore, the Presbytery of Cincinnati, acting under the authority of Jesus Christ, do hereby depose and exclude him from the office of a minister of the gospel, and do prohibit him from exercizing henceforth any of the powers and duties of that office."

But a part of his old congregation remained loyal to Dr. McCrackin, and they have organized a new community church, in which he now continues to function as their pastor. He has persisted in refusing to file, and no attempt has yet been made to collect from him. He has recently been visited by a federal agent, who asked him whether he still held the same views, to which he replied that he did.

And what is the author of this protest to do? I seem to be respected by the administration and was invited a few years ago to be present at some sort of official affair in honor of Henry Thoreau. I refrained from attending this and making a speech on the subject of civil disobedience. I should have liked to read aloud to the celebrators a passage which is cited by Dr. McCrackin in the autobiographical document quoted above and which is invoked by those peace organizations the descents of whose marchers on Washington are apparently so very unwelcome: "All men recognize the right of revolution; that is the right to refuse allegiance to and resist the government when its tyranny or its inefficiency are great and unendurable. But almost all say that such is not the case now. But such was the case, they think, in the revolution of 1775."

But I am not going to let myself be sent to Leavenworth, as Dr. McCrackin was. I have thought of establishing myself in a foreign country as my lawyer friend suggested and as I thought him rather absurd for suggesting. I do feel that I must not violate the agreement I have signed with the government to surrender for three years longer all the income that I take in above a certain taxable amount. My original delinquency was due not to principle but to negligence; but I now grudge every penny of the imposition, and I intend to outmaneuver this agreement, as well as the basic taxes themselves by making as little money as possible and so keeping below taxable levels. I have always thought myself patriotic and have been in the habit in the past of favorably contrasting the United States with Europe and the Soviet Union; but our country has become today a huge blundering power unit controlled more and more by bureaucracies whose rule is making it more and more difficult to carry on the tradition of American individualism; and since I can accept neither this power unit's aims nor the methods it employs to finance them, I have finally come to feel that this country, whether or not I continue to live in it, is no longer any place for me.

To one who was born in the nineteenth century, and so still retains some remnants of the belief in human progress of a moral as well as a mechanical kind, it is especially repugnant to be forced to accept preparations for the demise of our society or of a damage to it so appalling that it is impossible to see beyond it. The confident reformer of the past always saw himself confronted by an enemy, the defeat of whom would represent for him a release of the forces of life, the "dawn of a new day," the beginning of "a better world." But who today is the reformer's adversary? Not the trusts, the "malefactors of great wealth." Not "capitalism," not "communism." Simply human limitations so general as sometimes to seem insurmountable, an impulse to internecine destruction which one comes more and more to feel irrepressible. These elements, plus our runaway technology, have produced our Defense Department, with its host of secret agents and diligent bureaucrats of the Pentagon and the CIA, who have got themselves into a position where they have not merely been able to formulate policy without the approval of Congress but even to carry it out; with its pressure on Congress itself which enables it to get its vast appropriations granted; with its blackmail through bugaboo by which it makes the country live in constant terror of an invasion by Soviet Commissars; with its stimulus to the gigantic war industries, which give employment to so much labor, and its equipping of so many laboratories that give employment to technicians and scientists; with its discouragement of young men's ambitions by imposing on them two stultifying disruptive years of obligatory military service.

How to get rid of this huge growth, which is no longer a private organization, like one of Theodore

Roosevelt's old trusts that could be busted, that is not even a thriving corporation protected by a business administration but an excrescence of the government itself which officially drains our resources and which stupidly and insolently threatens our lives? In our day, the possibilities for human self-knowledge and for knowledge of the universe of which we are part, for the extension, both physical and mental, of human capabilities, have been opened up in all directions. We can not only fly and dive but are learning to live in space and beneath the sea; we are beginning to understand our relation to the other animals and our development as a genus among them; we have burrowed into the ruins of cities seven thousand years old and have had glimpses of the lives of men that existed many millennia earlier; we are coming to comprehend something about the processes by which we reproduce and by which our memories work; we have mastered techniques of the fine arts and other exploits of imaginative thought that lift us as far above our squalors as our space rockets do above the earth—and yet, skilled in and inspired by all this, we are now dominated by the great lethal mushroom that expands from the splitting of atoms and poisons the atmosphere of the earth and by the great human fungus behind it, which multiplies the cells of offices, of laboratories and training camps and which poisons the atmosphere of society. I should not make the mistake I have mentioned above of isolating a human institution and regarding it as the enemy of humanity. It is admitted that, in the phenomenon of hypnotism, the victim must have the will to be hypnotized; and we have now been hypnotizing ourselves. We have created the war branches of our government in one of our own images. But now that things have gone so far, is there any chance, short of catastrophe, of dismembering and disassembling this image and constructing a nobler one that answers better to what we pretend to?

All such images, to be sure, are myths, national idealizations. But there has been enough good will behind ours to make the rest of the world put some faith in it. The present image of the United States —homocidal and menacing—is having the contrary effect. And for all our boasts of wealth and freedom we are submitting to deprivation and coercion in order to feed and increase it.

Printed in the USA
CPSIA information can be obtained
at www.ICGtesting.com
LVHW091135150724
785511LV00001B/170

9 780374 526689